IV Mechanics
- 25 Italics
- 26 Capitals
- 27 Abbreviations
- 28 Numbers

V Stylistics
- 29 Finding a Style
- 30 Clichés
- 31 Tone
- 32 Simplicity
- 33 Euphony
- 34 Emphasis
- 35 Parallelism
- 36 Repetition and Synonyms
- 37 Variety
- 38 Specificity
- 39 Appropriate Diction

VI Fine Points
- 40 Writing the Introduction
- 41 Writing the Conclusion
- 42 "Sexist" Writing
- 43 Proper Manuscript Form
- 44 Usage

Index

THE CONTEMPORARY STYLIST

BRUCE BAWER

Harcourt Brace Jovanovich, Publishers
San Diego   New York   Chicago   Austin   Washington, D.C
London   Sydney   Tokyo   Toronto

Copyright © 1987 by Harcourt Brace Jovanovich, Inc.

All rights reserved. No part of this publication may be reproduced or transmitted in any form or by any means, electronic or mechanical, including photocopy, recording, or any information storage and retrieval system, without permission in writing from the publisher.

Requests for permission to make copies of any part of the work should be mailed to: Permissions, Harcourt Brace Jovanovich, Publishers, Orlando, Florida 32887.

ISBN: 0-15-513716-6
Library of Congress Catalog Card Number: 86-81619
Printed in the United States of America

About the Author:
Bruce Bawer is a literary critic who contributes regularly to the *New Criterion*. His essays and reviews have appeared in such publications as the *New York Times*, *Newsweek*, and the *London Review of Books*. The author of a critical study entitled *Middle Generation*, he holds a Ph.D. from the State University of New York at Stony Brook and lives in New York City.

Preface

The Contemporary Stylist is founded on the conviction that the greatest crime the author of a composition handbook can commit is to make writing seem a dull and formulaic activity—solely a matter of applying rules, of plugging in grammatical units. In accordance with this philosophy, I have tried to write a book that is at once comprehensive and succinct, responsible and stylish, informative and entertaining; a book that helps student writers realize that the purpose of composition rules is not to frustrate and confuse but to make possible the coherent expression of the individual human sensibility; a book that regards writing as a difficult but exhilarating process of discovery—a discovery of language, of ideas, of the world, of oneself.

I thank the reviewers: Samuel Bellman, California Polytechnic University; Eileen Evans, Western Michigan University; Philip O'Mara, Jackson State University (Michigan); John N. Snapper, Calvin College (Michigan); and David Yerkes, Columbia University.

For their help and advice on this project, I thank Nell Bawer, Erich Eichman, Sari Friedman, and Hilton Kramer—none of whom can be held responsible for its shortcomings. I also express gratitude to my editors, Paul H. Nockleby, Robert C. Miller, and Karen E. Lenardi, and my agent, Richard Balkin.

Contents

Preface   vii

I
The Paper   1

1 Finding and Narrowing a Topic   3
2 From Topic to Thesis   11
3 Organizing the Paper   19
4 Writing the Paper   31
5 Development   35
6 Unity and Topic Sentences   44
7 Coherence and Transitional Words   49
8 Revision   59

II
The Sentence   63

9 Parts of Speech   65
10 Sentences   74
11 Modifiers   80
12 Voice   85
13 Fragments   88
14 Comma Splices and Fused Sentences   93
15 Subject-Verb Agreement   96
16 Pronoun-Antecedent Agreement   107

III
Punctuation 111

17 Commas 113
18 Semicolons 124
19 Apostrophes 129
20 Quotation Marks 135
21 Period, Question Mark, Exclamation Point 144
22 Colon 149
23 Dashes, Parentheses, Brackets 153
24 Virgules, Ellipses, Hyphens 159

IV
Mechanics 163

25 Italics 165
26 Capitals 171
27 Abbreviations 176
28 Numbers 179

V
Stylistics 183

29 Finding a Style 185
30 Clichés 195
31 Tone 200
32 Simplicity 206
33 Euphony 212
34 Emphasis 216

    35 Parallelism   225
    36 Repetition and Synonyms   234
    37 Variety   244
    38 Specificity   255
    39 Appropriate Diction   263

VI
Fine Points   273

    40 Writing the Introduction   275
    41 Writing the Conclusion   284
    42 "Sexist" Writing   293
    43 Proper Manuscript Form   297
    44 Usage   309
    Index   325

I

The Paper

1

*'Fool!' said my Muse to me, 'look
in thy heart, and write!'*
—Sir Philip Sidney, *Astrophel
and Stella*

♦

Finding and Narrowing a Topic

"What should I write about?" That's the first question every writer faces, whether that writer is a Nobel prize-winning novelist, a student in a composition course, or Erma Bombeck. It's a question over which even the most experienced professional writers have been known to torture themselves and a question that many student writers, unfortunately, go about answering in the wrong way. "I should write about something *impressive*," the student writer tends to decide—which is another way of saying, "I should write about something I don't know about."

This is a bad idea. You can't do your best work on a topic chosen to "impress" your teacher. What you'll probably produce, if you take such an approach, is an uninspired paper on an overused theme—a paper that the teacher has seen (in one form or another) a hundred times before, a paper that has nothing in it of your personality, your intelligence, your way of looking at the world.

Remember that the point of any piece of writing is not to impress but to *communicate*—to draw the reader's attention to a set of facts, an idea, an opinion, or an experience. But a good piece of writing should communicate more than this: it should convey, through its style and tone, a strong sense of the writer's character, perspective, and sensibility. Thus the best sort of topic to choose is one that you are familiar with, have devoted some thought and attention to, and have something to say about.

And don't sell yourself short. There *are* topics about which you have something to say, topics that are perfectly appropriate for a college paper. Here's the best way to figure out what these topics may be. Forget, if you can, that you are looking for a college paper topic. Forget your teacher, forget whatever notions you may have of what he or she "wants" you to write, forget your fear of not getting a good grade. Instead, consider these questions. What were you doing or thinking about just before you started worrying over paper topics? What was the subject of the last really good conversation (or argument) that you had with a friend? What are you skilled at? What do you like to spend your time doing? What was the last thing you got excited over, angry about, or intrigued by? What was the most interesting thing that ever happened to you or that you ever did? The most interesting course you ever took, book you ever read? What news event has captured your attention? What was the subject of the last article or cartoon that you tore from a newspaper? If you think you have no talent for writing—what *do* you have talent for? The answers to one or more of these questions should provide the rough material for a suitable college paper topic.

Frequently, the topic you come up with in this manner may well be too large to be handled adequately in a short paper. If so, you should *narrow* the topic—preferably in a direction that makes you more comfortable. Assume, for example, that you've decided to write about the Vietnam War. Perhaps you are interested in the war because your uncle was a Green Beret, or your mother was a flower child, or you've made friends recently with a Vietnamese war orphan. There are several possible directions in which to narrow this topic.

But what are those directions? How do you

come up with them? One way is to consider the journalist's five **W**'s—**who, what, when, where,** and **why.** Thinking about the word *who*, for instance, in connection with the Vietnam War may lead you to ask yourself: "Who started the war? Who carried it out? Who were the leaders that made the decisions?" Famous names may come to mind: Presidents Johnson and Nixon, for example, and perhaps Ho Chi Minh and Nguyen Van Thieu. (If such names don't suggest themselves immediately, there's nothing wrong with looking up "Vietnam" or "Vietnam War" in an encyclopedia and finding some names there.) Once you have listed a few names, a thoughtful examination of that list should lead you to a good topic—perhaps the effect on the war of Ho Chi Minh's political career or the effectiveness of General William Westmoreland's military strategy.

What's a good topic for one student, naturally, may not be a good topic for another. Your best friend may be fascinated by military strategy, while the very phrase "military strategy" makes you feel like yawning. If this is the case, it's probably not the topic for you. Instead, keep hunting. Go through the other four *W*'s—and don't forget **how,** either. Think about beginnings and endings, about cause and effect: what *caused* the Vietnam War? What made it end? What were its lasting effects on American foreign policy, on the people of Vietnam? Allow your mind to wander into areas that may not be related to your topic in any obvious way. Look at the books on your shelf.

Finding and Narrowing a Topic 7

Seeing a biology textbook may remind you of the medical advances that came about as a result of the Vietnam War; a French textbook may suggest a paper about the Paris peace talks—both of which are fine topics.

Keep in mind that the more you know about a topic, the better you will be at coming up with ideas for narrowing that topic. So if you really don't know much about the Vietnam War, the best initial step might be to walk over to the library and read a couple of encyclopedia articles about it. Or, better yet, find the section of the library where the books on the war are kept and thumb through a few of them. Take notes. And always let your own interests be your guide.

As you come up with possibilities for narrowed topics, make a list of them. No two students will come up with the same list, but a typical student might wind up with something like this:

1. the causes of the Vietnam War
2. American military strategy in Vietnam
3. the experience of the American soldier in Vietnam
4. drugs and the Vietnam War
5. the Paris peace talks
6. the American antiwar movement

Even these topics are too broad. But they represent the first step toward a well-limited topic. Let's say you decide to write about the American antiwar movement. Fine. This, too, can be narrowed in a number of directions. Here are some possibilities:

1. the Chicago convention riots of 1968
2. the "draft dodgers" who fled to Canada
3. protest songs of the Vietnam War
4. the role of drugs in the peace movement

Interested in music? Then the best topic for you might be Number 3: the part that protest songs played in the antiwar movement.

Alas, there is always the possibility that what seems like a great topic to you may not seem quite so great to your instructor. (Rest assured that this problem does not afflict student writers only; professional writers are always having their suggestions for topics shot down by editors.) So whatever topic you eventually settle upon, it can't hurt to check it out with the teacher before you begin writing.

Sometimes a teacher will give you a general topic and expect you to narrow it. Often this topic will be utterly unfamiliar to you. But don't let that bother you. Whatever the topic may be, the chances are that you can come up with an angle that suits you, that allows you to exploit your own knowledge and interests. Say, for instance, that you're taking a course in French history and the teacher wants a paper on seventeenth-century France—a topic you know absolutely nothing about. Don't panic. What are you most interested in? Sports? Why not a paper on athletics in seventeenth-century France? This will require a good deal of research, of course, but so will any paper on seventeenth-century France. The point is that if you are interested in athletics to begin with, chances are you will be more interested in seventeenth-century French athletics than in some other aspect of seventeenth-century France. You will probably also be more confident while writing the paper, and this is important. Because when a writer is truly interested in a topic, *it shows*—and that interest makes the writing more interesting to its readers. A writer's self-confidence shows, too—it gives the piece a sense of authority, makes readers feel that they are learning from someone who really knows what he or she is talking about.

The best college paper topic, in short, can often be found right under your nose. A few years ago, a student of mine couldn't think of a topic for a final paper. She agonized over it for weeks. Then she realized she'd had it all along. During those agonizing weeks, she'd also been complaining to me about a newspaper article she'd read recently. In this article, an education "expert" complained that American college students should not be offered elective courses; rather, as in Soviet universities, they should be told what to study. The article angered my student. She enjoyed fashioning her own course schedule: it made her feel like an adult, and it allowed her to have a say in her own intellectual development.

Suddenly it occurred to her to write a rebuttal to the newspaper article. The paper she wrote was competently written and extremely convincing, largely because she was really interested in her topic and because she used her own experiences and those of her friends to support her arguments. The paper earned her an *A*.

◆

*Realize that college paper topics
are all around you.*

2

*And many a thought did I build
up on thought, / As the wild bee
hangs cell to cell.*
—Robert Browning, *Pauline*

◆

From Topic to Thesis

Now you have a topic. But a topic's not enough. Every paper requires not only a topic but a thesis—a central idea or proposition, a point that the author wants to make. "Protest Music and the Vietnam War" is a topic. But it is not a thesis. A thesis must be expressed in the form of a statement—a sentence that declares something. If you're writing an *expo-*

sitory essay (one that presents information, such as the average front-page newspaper article), a *narrative essay* (one that tells a story chronologically, such as a play-by-play newspaper account of a football game), or a *descriptive essay* (one that attempts to draw a picture of a person, place, or object, such as a travel article describing Westminster Abbey), the thesis statement should be a map of sorts that prepares the reader for the territory to be covered. If you're writing an *argumentative essay* (one that attempts to persuade the reader of the validity of a certain point of view, like a newspaper editorial arguing that the death penalty should be abolished), the thesis statement should present the hypothesis that you intend to prove. A paper with the topic "Protest Music and the Vietnam War" might have any one of the following theses:

> The songs of musicians like John Lennon, Joan Baez, and Bob Dylan played an important role in mobilizing student sentiment against America's involvement in the Vietnam War.
>
> The Vietnam protest songs of musicians like John Lennon, Joan Baez, and Bob Dylan may have seemed powerful at the time—but when one looks back upon them now, they seem awfully corny.
>
> The Vietnam protest songs of John Lennon, Joan Baez, Bob Dylan, and their contempor-

aries belong to a long tradition of using music as a vehicle for social protest.

In the 1980s, the Vietnam protest songs of John Lennon, Joan Baez, and Bob Dylan still have something important to say to us about love, peace, and understanding among all people.

By taking a simplistic, self-righteously "moral" stand on the issue of American involvement in Vietnam, the protest songs of John Lennon, Joan Baez, and Bob Dylan served to discourage serious individual thought, on the part of American youth, about a very complex issue.

The *topic*, in short, determines the area you are going to cover; the *thesis* determines the route you are going to take through that area. Without a thesis a paper inhabits a certain territory, but is likely to drift aimlessly like a purposeless vagrant. However interesting or well-written such a paper may be, a reader cannot help but wonder: What's the point? How does all of this connect? What am I supposed to come away with? A sharply focused thesis gives a paper direction, gives it a goal to aim for. If you find, in the course of writing a paper, that you are unsure of which way to turn or what to say next, chances are you don't really have a sharply focused thesis to point the way.

For example, you may sit down to write a paper on that tired old subject, "What I did last summer."

14   *The Paper*

One of the many problems with this topic is that, unless you spent it with Madonna or Prince, nobody *cares* what you did last summer—at least not when you approach it that way. Another problem is that "What I did last summer" is not an actual thesis; it's just a topic. Yet an interesting paper—interesting to the reader *and* to you—can be fashioned from your summer memories if only you dig through them in search of a good thesis. Let's say you spent a week at the beach, and put together the following notes on the experience:

1. played beach games—volleyball, and so forth. Sprained my arm, had weird experience in hospital emergency room
2. went body surfing—risky but fun! A natural high
3. had a sense of freedom, but got restless toward the end
4. slept in the sun—got a tan. I know it's dangerous to take in all those rays, but it's hard to resist the social pressure to get a tan
5. had a summer romance, just like in old songs—Beach Boys, "Summer Love" from *Grease*, "Will I See You in September?" and so forth.

A number of interesting thesis statements, each of which leads to an entirely different kind of paper, could be derived from this list. Here is one example:

> Whether we admit it or not, many of us suffer nowadays from a harmful addiction to ultraviolet rays.

The temptation of many a beginning writer might be to support this thesis statement by running to the library and looking for government studies, charts, or surveys on the number of Americans who tan themselves without regard to the possibility of contracting skin cancer as a result. But this is not the best thing to do. To be sure, a few telling and well-placed statistics about the sales of suntan lotion and the rate of occurrence of skin cancer can be informative and convincing; but the most interesting way of supporting this thesis is to speak from your personal experience. Talk about yourself, about people you know, about people you met and saw at the beach last summer. Talk about your friend who spent the summer holding the sun reflector under his chin; about the woman who held her head a certain way all day, every day, just to catch the rays at the best angle; about the people at that Labor Day party who kept complimenting each other on their tans, as if it were a truly impressive accomplishment to have stimulated the production of melanin by lying in the sun for a couple of weeks. A what-I-did-last-summer essay of this sort can be witty, appealing, even thought-provoking. A thesis makes all the difference.

Somewhere near the beginning of your paper, you should give some indication of what your thesis is. You may want to state it explicitly in the very first sentence:

> It became clear to me this summer that, whether we admit it or not, many of us suffer nowadays from an almost obsessive need for massive doses of ultraviolet rays.

As I say, that's *one* way. Is it the right way for this paper? I don't think so. It's too blunt, dull, and unimaginative. Yes, it makes your purposes clear from the start, but it also makes a potentially entertaining paper sound very boring. What, then, can you do if you want to avoid this kind of opening? You can, instead, begin the paper by suggesting your thesis indirectly and can put off a specific statement of that thesis until the end of the paper—or, at least, until the end of the first paragraph. You might open the paper on tanning, for instance, with the following sentence:

> One of the most noteworthy things about my week at Myrtle Beach last summer was the number of people whose main interest seemed to be in acquiring a gorgeous tan.

Still boring? If you think so, you might choose instead to start off with a description of one of your tanning freaks. Draw a picture *first*, in other words, to capture your reader's attention, and then work your way around, as smoothly as possible, to your thesis:

> Let's call him Scott. He looked like a Scott. Early each morning he came to the beach clad in a pair of tiny red bathing trunks, lay on the sand ten or twelve feet from me, and spent the next six hours splayed out there with wet pieces of Kleenex over his eyelids, a solar reflector under his chin, and a solemn expression on his face that announced to one and all that tanning was a serious business.
>
> Scott—so intent was he upon his serious business that I never did find out his real name—was an extreme example, perhaps, but not all that extreme. The fact is, there are an awful lot of us around who suffer from an excessive devotion to ultraviolet rays. . . .

And so on. In this case, as you can see, the paper's thesis is not stated until the second sentence of the second paragraph. This is not necessarily a good or a bad location for a thesis statement; it just happens to be a good position for the thesis statement in *this* paper about *this* particular topic. Nevertheless, the thesis statement should usually appear somewhere within the first two paragraphs of a paper; quite often the end of the first paragraph turns out to be the best place for it.

But whether you choose to begin with a thesis statement or to hold off until a bit later in the paper, make certain, before you write word one of your paper, that you know exactly what your thesis is. Knowing your thesis from the start, and keeping it in mind with every sentence that you write—even if you don't state the thesis directly till the end of the paper—will make it much easier for you to write a good, clear, sharply-focused essay that your reader will be able to follow, to learn from, and to enjoy.

◆

Know your thesis from the start.

3

... there is a music wherever there is a harmony, order, or proportion. ...
—Sir Thomas Browne, *Religio Medici*

◆

Organizing the Paper

The ideas that lead to the choice of a topic—and, in turn, to a specific thesis—are usually disorganized and undeveloped. So once you have settled upon a thesis, the first task is to put those ideas in order. Make no mistake: in writing, there is no such thing as too much order. Readers get mixed up easily, much more easily than you may imagine. The slightest departure from a clear, simple logical progression of ideas can throw them into confusion. You must, therefore, organize your ideas as simply and clearly as possible.

Does this mean you should prepare a formal written outline? That depends. Few professional writers bother to create elaborate outlines with Roman numerals and subheadings and so forth. This is because successful professional writers create outlines in their minds: they know what they want to say—in other words, they have a clear thesis—and they have a pretty good idea of how they are going to develop that thesis, paragraph by paragraph. If you are capable of doing this, don't bother with a formal outline; if not, perhaps it is better to prepare one. You may not see any value in constructing an elaborate diagram, but you should at least jot down a few subtopics in the order in which you plan to cover them.

There are several basic approaches to organizing a paper. Assume you have decided to write a paper on the tanning phenomenon, as described in the previous section. One way to organize this paper is by **example**—by providing, that is, one illustration after another of the phenomenon at work: your friend with the solar reflector, the people at the party with their effusive compliments for each other's tans. Another method is by **classification**—by identifying and describing, in turn, three or four distinct types of tanning fanatics (assuming, of course, that there are indeed "types" of tanning fanatics). A third possibility is **comparison and contrast;** you could, in other words, devote the entire paper to a comparison of the tanning phenomenon with another contemporary craze—dieting, "fitness," or what-have-you. You can use **process analysis,** in which you describe, step-by-step—devoting a paragraph or so to each step—how tanning fanatics manage to achieve perfect tans (for instance, they wear skimpy bathing suits, purchase effective tanning lotion, use solar reflectors, roll over every fifteen minutes, and so forth). You can opt for a **cause and effect** approach, concentrating upon the various reasons behind people's obsessions with getting a tan. You can organize your paper by means of **definition:** what *is* tanning-mania? You can try **description:** how does the average tanning fanatic look and behave? Or you can select **narration:** relate, in chronological order, your personal observations of tanners throughout a single day at the beach.

Which of these methods should you use? That's for you to decide. In most cases, a brief examination of the preceding list will rule out one or more of the topics. If you don't honestly think there are distinct types of tanning fanatics, for instance, you would certainly not choose the classification route. Nor must you stick to a single method of organization; the essay that does so, to the exclusion of all other methods, is a rare one. Most essays, in fact, combine several of these approaches (just try to find a good essay that does not make use of example, description, or narration). In most well-organized essays, however, one method clearly predominates and determines the overall structure of the piece.

For obvious reasons, essays with different approaches may require thesis statements that, although they amount to pretty much the same thing, take somewhat different forms. By choosing a certain method of organization, therefore, you may also be choosing to alter—and, in some cases, refine—your original thesis statement. Take the original thesis statement for the tanning essay, for example:

> Whether we admit it or not, many of us suffer nowadays from a harmful addiction to ultraviolet rays.

A *comparison-and-contrast* essay on this topic would probably call for a new thesis statement—something like this, perhaps:

> Many Americans today suffer from a mania for tanning that in many ways resembles the current mania for dieting.

A *process analysis*, meanwhile, would require a thesis statement along the following lines:

> Many Americans are desperate to get a tan, and submit themselves to a complicated and boring procedure in order to do so.

The thesis statement of the tanning essay as originally formulated is suitable for a paper developed

Organizing the Paper 23

through example, definition, description, and/or narration.

Let's say you have decided on *comparison and contrast:* you want to compare tanning to fad dieting. The next step is to sketch the major similarities and differences between the two phenomena. Just brainstorm, without worrying for the moment about putting your ideas in the best order or the most precise language. The list you create might look something like this:

1. Both tanning and fad dieting can be medically dangerous . . . excessive dieting (or badly designed diets) can cause illnesses; excessive tanning can cause leathery skin, and even lead to skin cancer.
2. Both tanning and fad dieting result from social pressures to look "beautiful."
3. Interesting that once upon a time being tan and thin had nothing to do with beauty at all . . . the ideal Renaissance woman (Mona Lisa, for one) was pale and plump. Tan, thin bodies in those days meant you were poor—forced to work in the sun all day and unable to feed yourself. You were a peasant.
4. Yet tanning carries none of the possible benefits of dieting. After all, if you lose weight, it can be good for you. But tanning

doesn't do anything for your health at all, does it?
5. Serious tanners, like serious dieters, engage in extreme forms of behavior, act like fanatics.

You have five points here. What to do next? Look them over. Ask yourself: Which are the most important points? Are there any so unimportant, or irrelevant, that you should omit them? (If the answer is yes, do so.) Are any of them redundant—that is, are two or more of the points essentially the same, only expressed in different ways? (If the answer is yes, keep only one version.) Are any two points really pieces of a single point? If so, combine them. This seems to be the case with Numbers 2 and 3, which might best be expressed as a single point:

> Both tanning and fad dieting result from social pressures to look beautiful—and the concept of beauty involved is a highly contemporary one.

So now you have four main points. In which order should you cover them? There are several schemes to consider—some of which are obviously inappropriate for this paper. There's the **spatial** method, which is more properly suited to a description; in describing a house, for instance, you'd go from room to room. There's the **chronological** method—discussing events in the order in which they occurred—which is appropriate to a narration.

There's the **least-important-to-most-important** method, in which arguments, ideas, reasons, examples, details—whatever your paper consists of—are arrayed in order of increasing significance or interest. (You wouldn't want to follow a **most-important-to-least-important** method any more than you'd want to watch a baseball game that grew duller and duller with every inning.) There's the **general-to-specific** method, whereby you present your thesis first, then go into specifics. And finally there's the **specific-to-general** method, whereby you give your examples first, then follow with a detailed presentation of your thesis.

The *specific-to-general* method is an especially effective one because it offers you the opportunity, first, to grab the reader's attention with vivid examples instead of an immediate assault with generalizations and, second, to make the reader feel as if he or she is watching you in the very process of inferring your thesis from the raw facts. Let's say you've chosen the specific-to-general method for your essay on tanning and dieting. You should begin, then, by describing the specific behavior of tanners and dieters (Number 5). From there, you should go on to make general observations about the two phenomena. Now, which generalizations should you present first? Why not follow a chronological order? Begin with your description of the historical background of the two phenomena (Numbers 2 and 3), and follow with your discussion of the medical problems that the two phenomena can produce. That leaves Number 4 for the end: your discussion of the one important difference between tanning and dieting. After you've done a bit more thinking about these four points, your rough list of ideas should resolve itself into an outline that reads more or less as follows:

> *Thesis:* Many Americans today suffer from a foolish mania for tanning that in many ways resembles the current craze for dieting.
>
> I. Serious tanners, like serious dieters, engage in extreme forms of behavior in the pursuit of "beauty"
>   A. Tanners' behavior
>   1. They wear skimpy bathing togs for maximum exposure to sun
>   2. They use solar reflectors
>   3. They select tanning lotions that promise a "fast, dark tan"
>   4. They use 15-minute alarm timers to signal when to turn over
>   B. Dieters' behavior
>   1. They buy every new diet book that comes along
>   2. In accordance with the instructions in these books, they construct elaborate menus, count every calorie, and shop with calorie lists in hand

3. They pick at their foods, removing the bread from sandwiches and icing from cake, etc.

II. The notions of beauty that tanners and fad dieters are trying so desperately to conform with are, in both cases, not eternal notions at all, but are characteristic rather of late twentieth-century America

  A. Being tan and thin used to be considered undesirable; pale and heavy was in style

   1. Pale skin and a certain heft were marks of beauty

      a. Medieval and Renaissance paintings portray ideal women (though not always ideal men) as pale and plump

      b. In writings from ancient Greece to the nineteenth century, the standard descriptions of female beauty include pale skin, never tan, and some poets bragged about their lovers' corpulence

   2. Tans and thinness were identified with poverty

      a. In the preindustrial age, only poor people routinely got tans (from working in the sun). Similarly, thin people were those unable to afford enough food

       b. Wealthy women carried parasols to avoid the sun, and were proud of their multiple chins
- B. The ideal of beauty that includes being tan and thin is a consequence of various twentieth-century American phenomena
    1. The idealization of tans results partly from industrialization: in late twentieth-century America, less affluent folk work not outdoors but in factories and such; tans are therefore not a sign of poverty but of affluence, with a good deal of outdoor leisure time available
    2. And the idealization of thinness results partly from the fact that many poor Americans nowadays do not eat too little but rather eat too many high-cholesterol, fattening foods; thinness is therefore not a sign of poverty but of affluence and enough education to eat "properly"
- III. Both tanning and dieting can be medically dangerous, and even ruinous of beauty
    - A. Problems caused by tanning
        1. Leathery skin
        2. Skin cancer
    - B. Problems caused by irresponsible dieting
        1. Gaunt appearance

      2. Acidosis and other abnormal conditions
IV. But tanning offers none of the possible benefits of dieting—sensible weight reduction can put years on your life, place less strain on your heart and lungs, give you more energy; tanning, though it may be psychosomatically beneficial, is invariably more harmful than helpful to one's health

If you examine this outline in detail, you will see that, within the specific-to-general framework, there are other organizational principles at work on lower levels. Sections II and III are in chronological order. The subheads under "Dieters' behavior" are also in chronological order: buy diet books, construct menus, follow them fanatically. And the medical ailments that can result from tanning and dieting are deliberately presented in least-important-to-most-important order, with "leathery skin," for instance, preceding "Skin cancer."

Notice that throughout the outline, discussion of a given aspect of tanning precedes discussion of the corresponding aspect of dieting. There is no reason why tanning should precede dieting. In most compare-and-contrast essays, the choice is completely arbitrary. But whichever order you decide upon at the start should be used consistently throughout the paper. To do otherwise would create unnecessary confusion. And remember: in all writing, confusion is the enemy and clarity the goal.

One last word about outlining. An outline cannot help but look extremely mechanical, with its I's and II's and A's and B's and so forth all so stiffly arrayed. The piece of writing that results from an outline, however, should look anything but mechanical. As an unseen skeleton gives a definite shape to a human body, so an outline, lurking beneath the supple contours of an essay's prose, should give a definite shape to an essay while itself remaining unseen. An essay whose outline protrudes too blatantly is a failed essay. So, by all means, *don't* hit the reader over the head with your organization. In other words, don't use expressions like "My next point is" or "The following examples illustrate this idea." For the first instance, "Moreover" or "Furthermore" would probably do just as well; for the second, "For example" or "For instance" are equally adequate.

Don't think, either, that once you have settled upon your outline you've done most of the work. Not at all! Your work has just begun. Writing is not a science but an art. It is easy to turn a good outline into a paper; what is difficult is to turn an outline into a well-written, interesting, and persuasive paper.

◆

Whether or not you use a formal outline, always know where you're going.

4

*The truth is that writing is a
blood sport, a walk in the garden
of agony every time out....*
—Craig Vetter, quoted in *The New York
Times*

◆

Writing the Paper

Now that you have an outline, you're ready to write. But don't be a slave to your outline. This is a mistake made by many beginning writers, who follow their outlines obsessively and end up with something so mechanical that it lacks both personality and style. You must not, in other words, let your outline stifle your imagination and wit. *Be flex-*

ible. Writing is an improvisational process; it is more like dancing or playing jazz music than it is like building a house by blueprint. Builders can rarely abandon their blueprints; but every writer should be ready, any moment, to restructure a piece of writing from the ground up. For instance, if in the course of writing you come up with new ideas (new arguments for your position, new reasons to support an argument) or if you figure out a more useful way of organizing your paper, you should be ready to make whatever changes are necessary. Don't become immobilized by the scope of the changes. In order to produce the best possible paper, you must be willing to do whatever is necessary. Few professional writers complete a piece of writing without sooner or later resorting to the scissors-and-tape method—in other words, cutting up the manuscript, reorganizing it, writing new transitions to tie the parts together again, deleting paragraphs, and refocusing. Many writers do this again and again until they are satisfied, until everything seems to come together to form a well-orchestrated whole. It's not easy. In fact, in its own way writing—*good* writing, anyway—is as much a test of endurance as an Olympic marathon.

And, as with a marathon, you have to go it alone. Teachers and books can help train you—they can show you how to find topics, organize ideas, avoid grammatical and mechanical errors, and document sources. But that's where their part in the process ends. For when all is said and done, *you* have to write the paper—*alone*. No one can lead you through this; no one can stand by your side and show you how to do it. Whatever problems arise in turning the vague, unformed ideas in your head into clear, coherent sentences on the page, you must solve them by yourself.

Writing, in short, is a lonely act. This fact disturbs many beginning writers; nowadays many people are not comfortable with the idea of being alone with their feelings and ideas. (*Really* alone—no MTV, no headset.) The notion of sitting in a quiet room, alone with their own thoughts, is enough to scare some of these folks away.

The thing to remember—the thing that most beginning writers don't even realize—is that the problems you have with writing are the same ones that even the great writers have had. For great writers, too, sit at their desks feeling stupid, unable to think, convinced that the few ideas they have are worthless and that they are incapable of putting together a simple sentence. Don't make the mistake of thinking that your problem is a lack of talent; too many beginning writers defeat themselves from the start in this way. They produce a few bad sentences and tell themselves, "I've got no writing talent; this is the best I can do." And they give up. Yes, there is such a thing as writing talent; but you don't need it to turn out a good—or even an excellent—English composition. What you need most of all are patience and an ability to concentrate. You must be willing to sit down and think about nothing except a single, tightly focused topic for several hours in a row, perhaps several days in a row. You have to do this knowing that the result will be a two- or three-page composition that someone else will take a minute to read; you have to do it knowing that no one except you will ever realize what anguish and self-doubt, sweat, and confusion went into turning those vague, clumsy thoughts of yours into a few paragraphs of clear, readable prose. That's the way it works—and it doesn't matter whether you're Flannery O'Connor or a student in freshman comp.

◆

*Don't let the difficulties and
frustrations of writing defeat you.*

5

So slow / The growth of what is excellent.
—William Cowper, *The Task*

◆

Development

Trying to turn your outline into an essay can be perplexing. You've got a handful of main points—but how do you actually turn them into an essay? The answer is to develop the main points by one means or another, assigning each main point at least one paragraph. There are several strategies for developing a paragraph—and they are the same strategies, applied on a smaller scale, as those available for organizing a paper: *example, classification, comparison and contrast, process analysis, cause and effect, definition, description,* and *narration.* It doesn't matter what strategy you use to organize the paper as a whole; a given paragraph within the paper may be developed through any strategy that strikes you as appropriate.

Here are a couple of illustrations from essays by well-known writers. An essay entitled "Barry Goldwater: A Chat," by Gore Vidal, takes a narrative approach overall: it is structured around an interview that Vidal held with Goldwater, and it tells how the interview progressed from question to question. But in one paragraph there is no narrative at all. Instead, in this one paragraph Vidal develops his point by the use of *example.* The paragraph's point is that contemporary American politicians must conform to certain conventions. Vidal develops this point, simply enough, by telling us what some of these conventions are:

> Like his predecessors, an American politician, in the mid-twentieth century, must conform to certain conventions. He must be gregarious (or seem to be), candid (but never give the game away), curious about people (otherwise, he would find his work unendurable). An American politician must not seem too brainy. He must put on no airs. He must smile often but at the same time appear serious. Most disagreeable of all,

according to one ancient United States Senator, wise with victory, "is when you got to let some s.o.b. look you straight in the eye and think he's making a fool of you. Oh, that is gall and wormwood to the spirit!" Above all, a politician must not sound clever or wise or proud.

The preceding illustration offers a good example of paragraph development. If you read through any published essay, however, you will find that few paragraphs are developed as straightforwardly as Vidal's. And who would *want* them to be? After all, if every paragraph of Vidal's essay consisted of an assertion followed by a list of examples, it would make extremely dull reading.

The average paragraph, therefore, tends to mix its methods. A good example is found in Jan Morris's essay, "Los Angeles: That Know-How City." Morris's essay is, on the whole, descriptive; her main purpose is to paint a vivid and realistic picture of life in Los Angeles. And so most of the essay is concerned with conjuring up images of the splendors of the Hollywood hills, Sunset Boulevard, a TV studio. But there is one paragraph in the essay which Morris develops in three different ways, none of them descriptive:

> Los Angeles, in the generic sense, was a long time coming. It is not a young city. Spaniards were here before the United States was founded, and I never get the feeling, as

> I wander around L.A.'s vast, amorphous mass, that it lies thinly on the ground. It is not like Johannesburg, for instance, where almost within living memory there was nothing whatsoever. Nor does it feel transient or flimsy, like some of those towns of the Middle West, which seem to have no foundation at all, but await the next tornado to sweep them away in a tumble of matchwood. In Los Angeles there are reminders of a long tradition. There is the very name of the city, and of its euphonious streets and suburbs—Alvarado, El Segundo, Pasadena, Cahuenga Boulevard. There is the pattern of its real estate, still recognizably descended from the Spanish and Mexican ranches of long ago. There is its exotic taste in architecture, its patios and its deep eaves, its arcades, its courtyards. There are even a few actual buildings, heavily reconstructed but still authentic, which survive from the first Spanish pueblo—swarmed over by tourists now, but fitfully frequented too, I like to think, by the swaggering ghosts of their original caballeros.

Morris's main point is that Los Angeles is an old city, as American cities go. One way in which she develops this point is by **repetition**—a method which I have not mentioned, but which (when handled carefully and elegantly) can be effective in reinforcing a major idea. Morris states this paragraph's major idea no fewer than three times at the paragraph's beginning. In the first sentence, she says that Los Angeles "was a long time coming"; in the second, that "it is not a young city"; in the third, that the city does not lie "thinly on the ground." These are three different ways of saying the same thing—but it works because they *are* different ways, because the rhythm works (the first sentence is medium length, the second short and punchy, the third long and thoughtful), and because the point bears repeating. In the fourth and fifth sentences of her paragraph, Morris develops her point further by using comparison and contrast: she contrasts Los Angeles with younger cities like Johannesburg and with towns in the American Midwest that seem to have neither a past nor a future. And in the remainder of the paragraph, she develops her point even further by using examples: she discusses streets and buildings that testify to the age of the city.

Seasoned professional writers like Vidal and Morris, of course, usually don't have to think consciously about how to develop a paragraph. When it came time to write about the age of Los Angeles, for instance, Morris probably didn't say to herself: "Hmm, I think I'll begin with repetition, then move on to comparison and contrast, and end up with examples." The development of the paragraph just came naturally. But if developing a paragraph doesn't come naturally to you—or if a specific paragraph is giving you trouble—your best bet is to look through the list of development strategies and think about which would be most suitable.

Assume, for example, that you have to write a paragraph on the following topic: "Frank Sinatra has been an important figure in American entertainment for more than forty years." How do you make a paragraph out of this? You might develop it by using *examples* of Sinatra's record of achievement as an entertainer:

> Among the highlights of his career are his Oscar-winning performance as Maggio in the celebrated *From Here to Eternity*, his song-and-dance escapades with Gene Kelly in *On the Town*, and his portrayal of a World War II soldier in the adventure film *Von Ryan's Express*.

Or you could try *classification*, breaking down Sinatra's show business activity into a number of categories:

> He has been a band singer, with the swing bands of Harry James and Tommy Dorsey. He has been a movie actor, in films like *It Happened in Brooklyn* and *Young at Heart*. He is, in his own words, a "saloon singer," entertaining at places from the Sands Hotel in Las Vegas to New York's Carnegie Hall.

Or you could use *comparison and contrast*—comparing Sinatra to other entertainers who have succeeded as grandly or lasted as long and contrasting him with those who haven't:

> Few show business figures have enjoyed such extreme and enduring popularity. To be sure, ten years after Sinatra's fame peaked, Elvis was equally successful, and ten years after that the Beatles were too. But Elvis is dead and the Beatles are history; and Frank Sinatra is still going strong. Other crooners from the forties, such as Tony Martin, have faded into near obscurity; and most of the still-living movie stars of that era, such as Marlene Dietrich and Greer Garson, have been retired for a long time. Only a tiny handful, like Katherine Hepburn, have continued, along with Sinatra, to make a vital contribution to contemporary entertainment.

Or *narration:*

> Sinatra's full-scale popularity began in 1942 with his recording of "I'll Never Smile Again." Within a couple of years he was singing at the Paramount Theater in New York, where he drew mobs; and by the end of World War II he was the premier recording artist in the country. . . . [And so forth.]

The preceding forms of development all seem to apply naturally to the Sinatra paragraph. But how about *description*? Here's a possibility:

> The setting is the Kennedy Center in Washington, D.C.—a huge, glittering auditorium

filled with the famous and powerful. The men are wearing tuxedos, the women expensive gowns. At the place of honor in the first balcony are President Reagan and the First Lady. Beside the First Lady stands a sixty-odd-year-old man with a round, gold-colored medal hanging from his neck. It is Frank Sinatra. He, along with four other Americans, is being honored here for his lifetime contribution to the American arts.

We have now developed our topic—the enduring importance of Frank Sinatra as an entertainer—in five different ways. We have generated more than enough material to construct a well-developed paragraph on this topic. The task now is to decide which material is the strongest and to combine it, in an intersting and forceful way, to create the paragraph. The result might be something like this:

> Ever since the early forties, when the sound of his voice made girls scream and faint—as Elvis would do ten years later, and the Beatles twenty years later—Frank Sinatra has been a compelling figure in American entertainment. He began as America's most popular vocalist, the boy singer with the famous swing bands of Harry James and Tommy Dorsey; he went on to become one of the world's favorite movie actors, in such films as *On the Town* and *From Here to Eternity*, for which he won an Oscar; and in recent years he has become *the* ultimate

show business legend, whose performances at such places as the Sands Hotel in Las Vegas and New York's Carnegie Hall never draw anything less than a sellout crowd.

This is not the only way to develop this paragraph. There are several other ways—and some of them would surely be just as acceptable. (Here's an exercise: write a paragraph of your own that develops this same topic.)

◆

Develop every major point adequately.

6

. . . the essay must be pure—pure like water or pure like wine, but pure from dullness, deadness, and deposits of extraneous matter.
—Virginia Woolf, *The Common Reader*

◆

Unity and Topic Sentences

Every paper should have **unity:** it should stick to one topic and focus upon one thesis.

Paragraphs should have unity, too. Each paragraph, in other words, should have its own central idea; it should *add* to, *not repeat*, what you have said in preceding paragraphs. In the course of the paragraph, you should not deviate from that central idea.

Many beginning writers cannot help including anecdotes, descriptions, jokes, and "impressive" words or phrases in paragraphs where they don't really belong. If you are such a beginning writer, carefully examine your rough drafts for anything that distracts a paragraph from its topic for as much as a single sentence. It doesn't matter if it's the funniest joke, the most interesting story, the best sentence you've ever written. If it doesn't belong, *omit it.*

As you probably know, a paragraph's central idea may be expressed in the form of a **topic sentence.** Often, as in the following paragraph from Shiva Naipaul's essay "The Road to Nowhere," the topic sentence may be placed at the beginning of the paragraph:

> Hull, in the middle of the winter, is a sobering place. Chill winds, blowing off the North Sea, sweep unhindered through the town. A persistent drizzle nags. The Humber, its unfinished suspension bridge rearing into the mist, is a steely blur. Lymphatic faces peer from under dripping umbrellas. By seven in the evening, the town is largely deserted, abandoned to the wind and rain. Roaming in bands of three or four, platformed heels echoing through the emptiness, the young hurry along the glistening streets in search of diversion. In the bars of the Centre Hotel commercial travellers occupy the mock-leather armchairs, warming themselves with scotch.

Every sentence of Naipaul's paragraph (except perhaps the last) serves to illustrate the idea that "Hull, in the middle of the winter, is a sobering place."

Yet the topic sentence doesn't have to come at the beginning. It can come in the middle, at the end—wherever it seems most naturally to belong. Say you're writing a paper about your friend Jim, in which you are trying to establish how eccentric he is. You've decided that in one paragraph of this paper you will describe his dormitory room, since you recognize that the room in which a person lives can tell a good deal about that person. In the first draft of your paper you may, in the usual fashion, put the topic sentence at the beginning of the paragraph:

> Jim's dorm room is as eccentric as Jim himself. The walls are bare except for two expensively framed portraits which Jim says are two hundred years old. These paintings stare at each other from opposite walls. The bed is always neatly made, and the books (most of them studies of obscure Oriental religions and dictionaries of Tibetan, Tagalog, and other exotic languages) are neatly placed on the bookshelf. There are no socks on the floor, no papers on the desk, and the typewriter is always covered—with a two-hundred-year-old horse blanket bearing Jim's ancestral coat of arms.

While writing the second draft of this paper, you may decide that the placement of the topic sentence at the beginning of the paragraph is too blunt or that you have too many paragraphs in a row that begin with topic sentences. Or perhaps you simply feel that you could improve upon the paragraph. You may, for instance, choose to open it with a touch of *compare-and-contrast* before proceeding to the examples:

> Most of our rooms in the dorm look exactly alike. There are the usual textbooks piled on our desks, the usual clothes on the floor; dirty socks accumulate under our beds; unframed posters and cheap art prints hang on our walls. Jim's room is another story entirely. His walls are bare except for two expensively framed eighteenth-century portraits that stare at each other from opposite walls. The bed is always neatly made, and the books (most of them studies in Oriental religion and philosophy, and dictionaries of Tibetan, Tagalog, and other exotic languages) are placed neatly on the bookshelf. There are no socks on the floor, no papers on the desk, and the typewriter is always covered—with a horse blanket that's been in Jim's family for generations. This room, in short, is the perfect reflection of its wonderfully different resident.

The topic sentence here is the last one: "This room, in short, is the perfect reflection of its wonderfully different resident."

Let's say that, while writing your third draft, you decide that the topic sentence is unnecessary and that the paragraph works better if it ends with the horse blanket. Is this acceptable? Yes. Every paragraph must have a topic, but some paragraphs simply do not need a topic sentence. After all, sometimes the topic of a paragraph is so clear that to state it bluntly would ruin the paragraph's effectiveness, and might even make it seem silly. In the above excerpt, for example, the point of the paragraph—that Jim's room reflects his odd personality—is so obvious that a topic sentence is unnecessary. The paragraph would probably be more effective if it ended with the word "generations."

You may, then, omit topic sentences on occasion. But remember: never do so unless the paragraph in question is so well unified that the reader could easily write a topic sentence for it if asked to do so.

◆

Focus every paragraph on a single subtopic.

I cannot make it cohere.
—Ezra Pound, *The Cantos*

♦

Coherence and Transitional Words

Besides unity, a paragraph should have **coherence.** In other words, one sentence should flow clearly and logically into the next. There are several established ways of achieving this. One simple way is to repeat the paragraph's key word. Consider, for example, this paragraph about symbolism from Herbert Read's *The Philosophy of Modern Art*, in which I have italicized the words *symbol, symbolic,* and *symbolism* each time they appear:

> The true understanding of art depends upon an appreciation of the nature and uses of *symbolism. Symbolism* is one of the two ways in which the human mind functions, the other being the direct experience of the external world (the "presentational immediacy" of sense perception). Since language itself is already *symbolism,* and the complicated forms of thought depend on a system of *symbols* such as we have in the science of algebra, it is natural to assume that there is something primitive and ineffective about the presentational immediacy of sense perceptions. This is far from being the case. It is much more difficult to be faithful to our direct experience of the external world than to "jump to conclusions" which are in effect *symbolic* references. The poet, said Gautier, is a man for whom the visible world exists; he wishes, by this definition, to exclude from art those secondary elaborations of perception involved in the use of *symbols.* As the poet is condemned to use the *symbolism* of language, the ideal would seem to be quixotic. (Nevertheless poetry continues to reveal a fundamental strife between imagism and *symbolism.*)

Unless one is extremely careful, of course, the extensive repetition of a single word can result in monotony. That's where pronouns come in handy.

Consider this paragraph by Lewis Thomas, in which I've put the word *termites*, and each pronoun referring to termites, in italics:

> *Termites* are even more extraordinary in the way *they* seem to accumulate intelligence as *they* gather together. Two or three *termites* in a chamber will begin to pick up pellets and move them from place to place, but nothing comes of it; nothing is built. As more join in, *they* seem to reach a critical mass, a quorum, and the thinking begins. *They* place pellets atop pellets, then throw up columns and beautiful, curving, symmetrical arches, and the crystalline architecture of vaulted chambers is created. It is not known how *they* communicate with each other, how the chains of *termites* building one column know when to turn toward the crew on the adjacent column, or how, when the time comes, *they* manage the flawless joining of the arches. The stimuli that set *them* off at the outset, building collectively instead of shifting things about, may be pheromones released when *they* reach committee size. *They* react as if alarmed. *They* become agitated, excited, and then *they* begin working, like artists.

Termites is the key word in this paragraph, and the eleven pronouns that refer to termites are Lewis's principal method of linking one sentence to the next.

An alternative to the repetition of a single key word is the use of several **synonyms** or **synonymous**

expressions. Consider the following paragraph, in which *wiretapping and bugging* appears four times:

> *Wiretapping and bugging* became legitimate tools of law enforcement in 1968 when Congress passed the Omnibus Crime Control and Safe Streets Act, which specifies they can be used by authorities, with court approval. Since that time, devices for *wiretapping and bugging* have been planted in houses, offices, churches and other places where people speak in confidence. Once authorized, *wiretapping and bugging* are difficult to limit, particularly when the wiretappers want to hear everything, as is often the case. The widespread *wiretapping and bugging* take a toll: they inevitably undermine the trust that people need to feel in order to speak openly, to work together effectively and to share intimacies freely.

The repetition of *wiretapping and bugging* in the preceding paragraph provides coherence, but is stylistically awkward. One solution to this problem is to replace these key words, in some instances, with synonyms or synonymous expressions. Here is the same paragraph, as actually written (in "The Intrusive Ears of the Law") by Herman Schwartz:

> *Wiretapping and bugging* became legitimate tools of law enforcement in 1968, when Congress passed the Omnibus Crime Control and Safe Streets Act, which speci-

fies they can be used by authorities, with court approval. Since that time, *electronic eavesdropping* devices have been planted in houses, offices, churches, and other places where people speak in confidence. Once authorized, *such intrusions* are difficult to limit, particularly when the wiretappers want to hear everything, as is often the case. The widespread *snooping into the private lives of Americans* takes a toll: it inevitably undermines the trust that people need to feel in order to speak openly, to work together effectively and to share intimacies freely.

The italicized expressions in the preceding paragraph—*wiretapping and bugging, electronic eavesdropping, such intrusions,* and *snooping into the private lives of Americans*—are all different ways of saying the same thing. They keep the paragraph's key idea before the reader without being tiresome about it.

Perhaps the most common means of achieving coherence is the use of **transitional expressions.** Consider the following excerpt from a student composition:

If we continue with nuclear energy, we will be hurting ourselves. Nuclear energy is too dangerous to use. So many accidents can occur. There may be an overload of nuclear wastes.

This paragraph is unified—it has a single topic—but it is not as coherent as it could be. The connections between sentences are clear enough after the reader examines them for a moment—but the reader should not have to examine them for a moment. The connections should be clear immediately; the reader should be able to follow the argument without having to pause to figure out how one sentence leads to the next. This problem can be solved by the use of the following two transitional expressions which I have italicized:

> If we continue with nuclear energy, we will be hurting ourselves, *because* nuclear energy is too dangerous to use. So many accidents can occur. *For example*, there may be an overload of nuclear wastes.

Note how these two transitional expressions clarify the logical connections in this paragraph and make it much easier to follow.

Many beginning writers, when taught to use transitional expressions, make the mistake of using them interchangeably. To do this, of course, is absolutely wrong. Every transitional expression has a particular meaning—it signifies a specific logical relationship between the sentence in which it resides and nearby sentences. Before deciding which transitional expression to use, therefore, you must determine what the logical relationship is between the sentence in question and those that surround it.

Some transitional expressions signify that the sentence in question is simply adding to the preceding sentence. Among these expressions are *and, again, also, besides, equally important, furthermore, in addition, moreover, too, for another* (when a preceding sentence begins with *for one thing*), *second* (when a preceding sentence begins with *first*), *next, last, in the second place* (when a preceding sentence begins with *in the first place*), *finally, what's more.*

> The study of philosophy, my uncle Bob told me, helps enhance one's understanding of the nature of existence. Besides, it looks good on a resume.

Similarly and *likewise* draw comparisons.

> Uncle Bob likes to advise me about my college career. Similarly, Aunt Helen enjoys offering tips on manners and grooming.

Words like *although, but, despite, even so, however, nevertheless, nonetheless, notwithstanding, on the contrary, on the other hand, regardless, still,* and *yet* indicate contrasts:

> My other aunt and uncle, however, tend to keep their opinions to themselves.

Such expressions as *for example, for instance,* and *to illustrate* are used to signal that an example of something just stated follows:

> For example, when I told Aunt Harriet and Uncle Al that I couldn't decide whether to become a sheep shearer or a bassoonist, Aunt Harriet said, "Whatever makes you happy, dear."

Such expressions as *that is, that is to say,* and *in other words* indicate a restatement in different words:

> Aunt Harriet and Uncle Al, I suspect, are indifferent to my fate. That is, I have the feeling they don't care what I do.

Indeed and *in fact* are used to indicate that you are amplifying an assertion:

> Indeed, I don't think they care about much of anything.

After all and *of course* are used to indicate a general logical continuity:

> After all, if I were really important to them, they wouldn't have sent me a birthday card addressed to "Occupant."

Accordingly, as a result, because, consequently, for, hence, since, then, therefore, thus are used to indicate cause and effect:

> Because my aunts and uncles are so extreme in their behavior, I don't spend too much time with them.

The expressions *granted* and *to be sure*—and, quite frequently, *of course*—are used to indicate that you are acknowledging a fact that may seem to contradict something that you just stated:

> To be sure, I do see them on holidays.

All in all, in brief, in conclusion, in short, and *to summarize* are used to indicate that you are concluding:

> All in all, I suppose I have a pretty average extended family.

There are also, of course, transitional expressions that indicate spatial relationships (*above, beyond, here, nearby, there*) and temporal relationships (*afterwards, as soon as, at last, at length, at that time, at the same time, before, earlier, eventually, formerly, immediately, in the meanwhile, later, meanwhile, now, presently, previously, shortly, simultaneously, since, so far, subsequently, then, thereafter, thereupon, until, when*). There are even transitional expressions (*at any rate, in any case*) to indicate that there is no strong logical connection between the sentences being linked:

> At any rate, they're my family, and I guess I love them.

All of these devices—the repetition of key words, the use of pronouns and synonyms, and the use of transitional expressions—are useful ones. It's important, though, not to go overboard. You don't want to repeat key words *too* often or to begin every sentence of a paragraph with a transitional expression. Sometimes paragraphs are more forceful without such expressions than with them. Consider the following passage from Ashley Montagu:

> The cultured man is free of prejudices. He does not indulge in prejudgment. He does not believe in the process of supporting emotional judgments with handy reasons. He will not make judgments on insufficient evidence, finding such practice repugnant to everything for which he stands, and he declines to accept any statement as true unless it can be verified.

Transitional expressions could very well be used here: *for example* could be placed at the beginning of the second sentence, and both the third and fourth sentences could begin with transitional expressions of addition (*also, moreover,* and the like). But Montagu's passage does not need any such help. It's quite coherent: the relationship between the sentences is clear enough without transitional expressions. To add them needlessly would only weaken a strong, effective piece of writing.

While some paragraphs, then, benefit from the application of the devices I've described, other paragraphs are better off without them. Rest assured that the more comfortable you become with these devices, the better sense you'll have of when they are necessary and when they aren't.

◆

Make certain every sentence flows smoothly and logically from its predecessor.

8

*Ev'n copious Dryden wanted, or forgot, / The
last and greatest art—the art to blot.*
—Alexander Pope, *Epistle II: To a Lady*

◆

Revision

Professional writers will tell you that revision *is* writing. Not till you get a first draft on paper can you begin to shape an essay into something that resembles your original vision of it.

There are no hard and fast rules about revision. Sometimes two or three drafts are enough to achieve a satisfactory final version; sometimes more than twenty drafts are necessary. One mark of good and experienced writers is their ability to recognize that a piece they are writing still needs work.

How do you go about revising? Once your first draft is written, put it aside for a few hours—or, if possible, a few days. Then give it a fresh read; read it as if someone else had written it. Ask yourself these questions: (1) Is it *unified?* That is, is the entire composition focused on a single topic, or does it drift from one thing to another? Does each paragraph focus upon a single subtopic? (2) Is it *coherent?* That is, does one paragraph lead into another clearly and smoothly? Does one sentence follow another clearly and smoothly? (3) Is it *logical?* That is, does your reasoning make sense? (4) Are your major ideas, arguments, observations, facts, descriptions well-developed? (5) Is the paper stylistically sound?

Since you're dealing with a first draft, the answer to most of these questions is likely to be "No." "The first draft of anything is s----t," Ernest Hemingway once said, in his memorable way, and it's a rule with few exceptions. First drafts are repetitious, meandering, awkward, vague; the sentences don't follow one another smoothly; some points are not sufficiently developed, others are too fully developed; and the ideas are likely to be inadequately formed or imprecisely expressed. The mark of skilled writers is the patience and diligence with which they apply themselves to the elimination of these weaknesses from subsequent drafts.

When you write, you must consider every word—concentrate all your thoughts and energies upon whatever you're writing. But when you revise, you must stand back from your work—from this infant that you've wrenched from your guts—and be impersonal, ruthless, coldblooded. Pretend that someone else wrote the paper; forget that a page took two days to write or that it's the best written part of the entire paper. If that page doesn't really fit in, *throw it out.* (Or, even better, put it aside. Two or three drafts later you may find a place for it after all.)

There may come a time, in the process of revision, when you feel unable to make any further judgments about your paper. When this happens, try reading the paper aloud to yourself. Do you find yourself stumbling over some sections of it? Perhaps that means they are awkwardly written. Imagine that someone is listening to you read the paper aloud: are there any sentences, phrases, words that you are reluctant to read because they sound silly, clumsy, embarrassing? If so, rewrite them—or, if possible, delete them.

Don't be discouraged by the number of revisions necessary to achieve a satisfactory final draft. Revision is, after all, a writer's way of perfecting his or her art. It's equivalent to a baseball pitcher practicing throws, an actor rehearsing, a guitarist working on chord changes. And, as with the baseball player, the actor, and the guitarist, it doesn't matter how much "practice" or how many "rehearsals" you require to get it right: the only thing that matters is the final product.

A smart writer does not resent the necessity for revision but, instead, is happy at the opportunity. The novelist Kurt Vonnegut, for instance, writes that he likes "the writing trades" precisely because "they allow mediocre people who are patient and industrious to revise their stupidity, to edit themselves into something like intelligence."

◆

Keep revising your paper till it is as good as you can make it.

II

The Sentence

9

No nourishment to feed his growing mind, / But conjugated verbs and nouns declin'd?
—William Cowper, *Ticocinium*

◆

Parts of Speech

There are eight different types of words; they are called **"parts of speech."** They are (1) nouns, (2) verbs, (3) pronouns, (4) adjectives, (5) adverbs, (6) prepositions, (7) conjunctions, and (8) interjections.

Nouns are the names we give to things. More specifically, they are the names we give to people (*boy, teacher, baby*), places (*city, street, farm*), objects (*house, bicycle, automobile*), conditions (*height, illness*), and concepts (*beauty, truth, life, death, evil*). **Proper nouns** are the names we give to specific things. A specific boy, for example, may be called *George*; a specific city, *Detroit*; a specific automobile, a *Mercedes*. Proper nouns, as these examples demonstrate, are capitalized.

Nouns may be singular, naming one thing (*boy, house*), or plural, naming more than one (*boys, houses*). Most plural nouns in the English language are formed, as are *boys* and *houses*, by adding the letter *s* to the corresponding singular noun. But some add *es*: the plural of *tomato*, for example, is *tomatoes*. Some singular nouns ending in *f* or *fe* lose those endings when they become plural, and add *ves*: *thief* and *life* become *thieves* and *lives*. A few common singular nouns have particularly unusual plurals: *man* becomes *men*; *child, children*; *foot, feet*; *tooth, teeth*; *mouse, mice*. Some nouns are the same in both singular and plural form: *deer, moose, sheep*. And many words, "borrowed" by English from other languages, form plurals according to the rules of those languages. In accordance with the rules of Latin, then, *formula* becomes *formulae*; *index, indices*; *focus, foci*; *medium, media*; and so forth. Similarly, in accordance with Greek pluralization rules, *analysis* becomes *analyses*; *crisis, crises*; *criterion, criteria*. And the originally French *bureau* becomes *bureaux*. (In many cases, in place of or in addition to the foreign plural, there is a plural that is formed according to the rules of English: *formulas, indexes, bureaus.*)

Verbs are the words we use to describe actions, occurrences, states of being—for instance, *eat, chew, weep, transcend,* and *be*. Often, when speaking of verbs, we use the **infinitive** form—in other words, the form in which the verb is preceded by the word **to:** *to eat, to chew,* and so forth. Another familiar form is the **gerund**—the **-ing** form of a verb: *eating, chewing*. Both the infinitive and gerund forms may function as nouns:

> *To err* is human.
>
> *Eating* is my favorite pastime.

Whereas any given noun has two basic forms—singular and plural—a verb (such as *to eat*) may take several different forms (*eat, eats, ate, eaten, eating*), depending on a combination of several different factors.

To begin with, verbs may vary according to **number**—that is, according to whether they describe one action or several. Notice the different forms that the verb *to eat* takes in the following sentences:

Singular	*Plural*
Aaron eats.	Aaron and Kay eat.

Verbs may also vary according to **person**—that is, according to who or what is performing the action described. In the **first person,** the action is being performed by the writer or speaker, alone or with others; in the **second person,** by the person or persons whom the writer or speaker is addressing; in the **third person,** by someone or something else:

	Singular	*Plural*
First Person	I eat.	we eat
Second Person	you eat	you eat
Third Person	he eats	they eat
	she eats	Aaron and Kay eat
	it eats	the dogs eat
	Aaron eats	
	the dog eats	

Verbs may also vary according to **mood**—that is, according to whether the writer or speaker is describing something as actually happening (the **indicative mood**), demanding that something happen (the **imperative mood**), or hoping, doubting, suggesting, or imagining that something may happen (the **subjunctive mood**). In the following three sentences, the verb *to be* is in the third person singular, but varies in form according to mood:

Indicative	Aaron *eats* lunch every day.
Imperative	Aaron, *eat* your lunch.
Subjunctive	I suggest that Aaron *eat* his lunch.

Finally, verbs can vary according to **tense**—that is, according to when the action, occurrence, or state of being is conceived of as taking place. Every verb has three "principal parts"—the **present** (*eat*), the **past** (*ate*), and the **past participle** (*eaten*)—from which its various tenses are derived. It is not essential to know the names of all these tenses, but it is important to use them all correctly. Here, then, are several sentences in which the verb *to eat*, in the third-person singular, changes form as it changes tense:

Present Indicative	Aaron *eats* lunch every day.
Past Indicative	Aaron *ate* eggs for breakfast.
Future	Aaron *will eat* dinner alone.
Conditional	If I asked him to, Aaron *would eat* dinner with me.
Present Perfect	He *has eaten* dinner with me several times.
Past Perfect	When he sat down to breakfast today, he *had eaten* two sandwiches already.
Conditional Perfect	He *would have eaten* even more, but he ran out of money.

Future Perfect	When he sits down to dinner tonight, he *will have eaten* a whole box of Oreos and two papayas since lunch.
Present Subjunctive	It is important to Aaron that he *eat* constantly.
Past Subjunctive	His late mother's hope always was that he *might eat* more sensibly.
Imperative	Aaron, *eat* some wheat germ!

For each of these tenses, there is also a corresponding **progressive** tense that contains the gerund form. For instance, the conditional progressive form of the verb *to be* is *would be eating*; the past perfect progressive form is *had been eating*.

Such combinations of verbs as *might eat* and *would have eaten* are examples of the use of **auxiliary verbs** (or "helping verbs"). The verbs that are commonly used as auxiliary verbs are *be (am, is, are, was, were, been), have (has, had), do (does, did), will (shall), may, might, must, can, would, should, could, may, ought to, used to*. The sentences "I *am* eating," "He *does* eat regularly," "I *have* eaten today," and "I *may* eat a sandwich" all make use of auxiliary verbs. The parts of an auxiliary verb may be separated within a sentence by other words:

Does Tim *like* me just the least little bit?

Suzy, I *do* not *have* the least little idea.

A **pronoun** is a word that has no fixed meaning itself but takes the place of a noun. *I, me, mine, myself, we, it, this, who, which, everyone* are all pronouns.

An **adjective** (*tall, ridiculous, handsome*) modifies a noun or pronoun. (The three **articles** in the English language—*the, a,* and *an*—are usually classified as adjectives.) When you speak of a "tall boy" or a "ridiculous movie," you are using adjectives to modify nouns. An **adverb** (*ridiculously, very, too, never*) modifies a verb, an adjective, or another adverb. If you say that a movie "ends ridiculously," you are using an adverb to modify a verb; if you say that the movie is "ridiculously long," you are using the same adverb to modify an adjective; if you say that it ends "very ridiculously," you are modifying that same adverb with another adverb.

A **preposition** usually indicates a relationship between two nouns; in the following sentence, for instance, the preposition *in* indicates the relationship between the nouns *boy* and *movie:*

The boy is *in* the movie.

Sometimes a preposition indicates a relationship between a noun and a verb. Here the preposition *down* indicates the relationship between the verb *ran* and the noun *road:*

The boy ran *down* the road.

The words *above, across, at, by, from, in, of, on, onto, over, through, to, under, until,* and *with* are among the more common prepositions. These prepositions can all be used to connect the noun *boy* to other nouns:

> The boy is *on* television.
> The boy *from* Indiana stole my watch.
> The boy *under* the table is named Rick.
> The boy *with* my brother plays the oboe.

Or they may be used to connect the verb *ran* to the same nouns:

> The boy ran *into* the television.
> The boy ran *across* Indiana.
> The boy ran *to* the table.
> The boy ran *from* my brother.

A **conjunction** (such as *and, but, or, after, if, when, yet*) connects phrases, clauses, or sentences. In the following sentence, the conjunction *then* connects two phrases, *to the table* and *to the television:*

> The boy ran to the table, *then* to the television.

In the following sentence, the conjunction *when* connects two clauses:

> The boy ran across the room *when* my brother called him.

And in the following example, the conjunction *but* connects two sentences:

> The boy ran across Indiana. But my brother won the race.

Conjunctions also connect two or more words that are the same part of speech and that function identically in a sentence. In the following sentence, for example, the conjunction *and* connects the nouns *brother* and *boy:*

> My brother *and* the boy both enjoy running.

◆

Know the parts of speech and their relationships to one another.

10

Herke what is the sentence of the wise....
—Geoffrey Chaucer, *The Man of Law's Tale*

◆

Sentences

Of the eight parts of speech, only two—a noun (or pronoun) and a verb—are required for a complete sentence:

> Dogs bark.

This is a complete sentence because it tells us something; it requires no additional words to say what it has to say. It is a **simple sentence.** *Dogs*, a noun, is the *subject* of the sentence; that is, it indicates the person, place, object, condition, or concept that the sentence is telling us about. *Bark*, a verb, is the *predicate* of the sentence; that is, it indicates what the sentence wants to tell us about the subject. This is all you need to form a simple sentence: a subject and a predicate.

The subject can consist of a single noun, as in the sentence "Dogs bark." Or it can consist of more than one noun:

Hounds and terriers bark.

Here the subject consists of three words: the nouns *hounds* and *terriers* as well as the conjunction *and*, which is there to connect them. A subject can also contain other types of words—adjectives, for instance, to modify the noun:

The dangerous wild dogs bark.

The subject of this sentence consists of the words "The dangerous wild dogs." *The* is an article, usually classified as an adjective, and *dangerous* and *wild* are both adjectives; all three words modify the noun *dogs*.

Similarly, the predicate may consist of more than one verb:

Dogs bark and howl.

Here the predicate consists of two verbs, *bark* and *howl*, as well as the conjunction *and*. Like a subject, a predicate can also include other parts of speech that, in one way or another, elaborate upon or modify the verb:

> The dangerous wild dogs bark at night, loudly and frighteningly, in the gloomy woods behind my parents' house.

The predicate here is "bark at night, loudly and frighteningly, in the gloomy woods behind my parents' house." *Loudly* and *frighteningly* are both adverbs that modify the verb *bark*. "At night," "in the gloomy woods," and "behind my parents' house" are all **prepositional phrases.**

The last quoted sentence, though rather long and involved, is still considered a simple sentence because it consists of a single clause. A **clause** is a sequence of words that contains a subject and a predicate. A **compound sentence** is one that consists of two or more clauses, usually connected by a **coordinating conjunction**—of which there are seven in the English language (*and, but, or, nor, for, so, yet*):

> Dogs bark and cats meow.
>
> Dogs bark, but cats meow.

In some compound sentences, the clauses are not connected by a coordinating conjunction:

> Dogs bark; cats meow.

These are all compound sentences. So is this:

> The dangerous wild dogs bark at night in the woods behind my parents' house, and my cat meows back.

The two clauses that form a compound sentence are called **independent clauses,** because each could stand alone—independently—as a separate sentence:

> The dangerous wild dogs bark at night in the woods behind my parents' house. And my cat meows back.

Two clauses may also be combined to form a **complex sentence.** In a complex sentence, one clause, the **main clause,** is *independent*; it may be a complete sentence on its own. The other clause is a *dependent* clause, and is *subordinated* to the main clause. To subordinate a clause—to turn it, in other words, into a dependent clause—one must connect it to the main clause by means of a **subordinating conjunction.** Among the subordinating conjunctions in the English language are the following:

after	once	till
although	provided	unless
as	since	until
because	than	when
before	that	where
if	though	while

The following are complex sentences:

> Though dogs bark, cats meow.
> When dogs bark, cats meow.
> Cats meow when dogs bark.

The main clause in all three sentences is "cats meow," which could be a sentence by itself. The subordinate clauses of these sentences, however, begin with subordinating conjunctions ("though" in the first sentence, "when" in the second and third), and therefore could not be sentences by themselves:

> Though dogs bark.
> When dogs bark.

The following is also a complex sentence:

> When the dangerous wild dogs bark in the woods at night behind my parents' house, my cat meows back.

The main clause here is "my cat meows back"; the rest of the sentence is the subordinate clause.

What's the difference between compound and complex sentences? In a compound sentence, the two parts usually carry equal emphasis. In a complex sentence, the main clause usually carries greater emphasis than the subordinate clause. Since the placement of emphasis is an important part of good writing, every writer should be comfortable with the idea of changing simple sentences to compound, compound to complex, and complex to simple.

There is also such a thing as a **compound-complex sentence.** This sort of sentence contains two or more main clauses and one or more subordinate clauses:

> After we go to bed, the dogs bark and the cats meow.

◆

Recognize simple, compound, and complex sentences, and be able to change sentences of one type to sentences of another type.

11

*They did their best to modify
their case....*
—George Gordon, Lord Byron,
Don Juan

◆

Modifiers

When one word in a sentence describes another, we say that it modifies that word. In the sentence, "Suzanne bought a brown Isuzu," for example, the word *brown* modifies *Isuzu*. In "She drove it home quickly," the word *quickly* modifies *drove*.

Phrases and clauses can also be modifiers. Consider the following sentence:

> Turning and turning in the widening gyre,
> the falcon cannot hear the falconer.

Here, the phrase *Turning and turning in the widening gyre* modifies *falcon*, which is the subject of the sentence. It is the falcon, in other words, that is turning and turning. The logic in the following sentence is similar:

> Applauding wildly, the audience jumped to
> its feet.

The words *Applauding wildly* modify the word *audience*. It is the audience, clearly, that is applauding wildly.

A modifier should immediately precede or follow the sentence element that it modifies. A **misplaced modifier** is a word, phrase, or clause that is not placed carefully enough in a sentence—it seems to be modifying the wrong term or it is hard to tell *which* sentence element it modifies. Consider this sentence:

> I only have eyes for you.

Here the word *only* is ambiguous. Does the writer mean that he alone—and nobody else—has eyes for the person he's writing to? If so, he should have written the following:

> Only I have eyes for you.

Or does he mean that he has eyes—and nothing else—for the person he's writing to? If so, he should have written this:

> I have only eyes for you.

Or (as is probably the case) does he mean that he has eyes for that person—and for no one else? If so, the sentence should read as follows:

> I have eyes for you only.

Besides *only*, there are other adverbs that must be placed with special care. They include *almost, even, hardly, just, merely, nearly,* and *scarcely.*

A **squinting modifier** is one that is placed between two sentence elements, and may be intended to modify either of them:

> That you could have forgotten me completely devastates me.

Does *completely* modify *forgotten* or *devastates?* If the former, the sentence may be rewritten as follows:

> It devastates me that you could have forgotten me completely.

If *completely* is meant to modify *devastates*, on the other hand, the sentence may be rewritten in this manner:

Modifiers 83

> That you could have forgotten me devastates me completely.

Or:

> It devastates me completely that you could have forgotten me.

Or:

> It completely devastates me that you could have forgotten me.

When the modified term is left out of the sentence, the modifier is called a **dangling modifier:**

> Applauding wildly, the actors took their bows.

Who is applauding here? Not the actors, one realizes, but the audience. But the word *audience* does not even appear in the sentence. This error can be rectified in a couple of ways. The dangling modifier can be converted into a subordinate clause:

> As the audience applauded wildly, the actors took their bows.

Or we can make the word *audience* the subject of the sentence, thereby placing it in the proper position in relation to its modifier:

> Applauding wildly, the audience watched the actors take their bows.

Here's another example:

> To make cookies, flour and eggs and sugar are needed.

Who is making cookies here? Not the flour and eggs and sugar, certainly; the sentence must be rewritten as follows:

> To make cookies, one needs flour and eggs and sugar.

◆

Place modifiers correctly.

12

Two voices are there....
—William Wordsworth, *Poems Dedicated to National Independence*

◆

Voice

When the subject of a sentence performs the action designated by the verb, the verb is said to be in the **active voice**:

> James wrote a paper about avocados.

Here, *James* is the subject, *wrote* is the verb. The same action described in this sentence can be related in the **passive voice**:

> A paper about avocados was written by James.

Here the subject is *paper*, but it is still James who is doing the writing.

The active voice is perceived by readers to be more forceful than the passive voice. Or, to rewrite the above sentence in the active voice: Readers perceive the active voice to be more forceful than the passive voice. Many writers, however, write frequently in the passive voice anyway. I suspect that some of them do so because, whether they realize it or not, they are afraid of being forceful—even when the subject is something as innocuous as avocados.

Sometimes, to be sure, the passive voice can be useful. When the performer of an action is not known, a passive construction is justifiable:

> Gunpowder was invented in China.

The passive voice is also appropriate when the writer has a legitimate reason for emphasizing the receiver of the action rather than the performer of the action:

> The movie *Gone With the Wind* was made in 1939.
>
> My cat Fluffy was run over by a Mack truck on the Golden State Freeway.

In the first of these two sentences, a passive construction is appropriate because the writer does not want to have to list the people responsible for making *Gone With the Wind*. In the second sentence, the passive voice is appropriate because the writer wants to give more emphasis to the cat than to the truck. (Words at the beginning or end of a sentence tend to receive more emphasis than words buried in the middle of a sentence.) To put this sentence in the active voice would actually weaken it, because both the truck and the freeway would receive more emphasis than the cat:

> A Mack truck ran over my cat Fluffy on the Golden State Freeway.

It is often possible, though, to find a way of directing emphasis in the desired direction *and* writing in the active voice:

> A Mack truck, on the Golden State Freeway, ran over my cat Fluffy.

Or even:

> My cat Fluffy had a fatal encounter with a Mack truck on the Golden State Freeway.

The lesson here, then, is that you should not use the passive voice routinely: stick to the active voice. On occasion, however, you may find, after some thought, that a passive construction is preferable for a given sentence. In such cases, act accordingly.

◆

Except in special instances, use the active voice.

13

'Tis but a part we see, and not a whole.
—Alexander Pope, *An Essay on Man*

◆

Fragments

A **fragment** is a cluster of words that is not a sentence but is punctuated as one. Most fragments are errors and should be corrected; they confuse the reader and make the writer look confused, too.

Consider this excerpt:

> Everything about *Dynasty* is terrible. The amateurish acting of Joan Collins, the stiff

> posturing of John Forsythe, and the ridiculous, melodramatic story line.

This excerpt is punctuated as two sentences. But only the first is really a sentence. It has the two things required for a sentence: a subject (*everything*) and a verb (*is*). The second "sentence" lacks a verb, and is therefore a fragment. It's an example of the most common type of fragment: the type that lacks a verb and is a logical part of the sentence that precedes it. This error can be remedied simply by changing the period at the end of the first sentence into a colon, thereby turning the two sentences into one:

> Everything about *Dynasty* is terrible: the amateurish acting of Joan Collins, the stiff posturing of John Forsythe, and the ridiculous, melodramatic story line.

This problem could also have been solved by adding a predicate, thereby turning the fragment into a sentence:

> Everything about *Dynasty* is terrible. The amateurish acting of Joan Collins, the stiff posturing of John Forsythe, and the ridiculous, melodramatic story line all contribute to its mediocrity.

Sometimes a group of words may contain a noun and verb, yet still not be a sentence. Usually the reason for this is that the writer has begun the "sentence" with a subordinating conjunction (such as *after, although, as, because, if, since, though, unless, until, when, where, while*) or a relative pronoun (*what, whatever, which, who, whoever, that*). In the following example, the second "sentence" is really a fragment:

> Danny wants to watch *Dynasty*. Although he knows that it is a terrible show.

Without the subordinating conjunction *although*, the fragment would be a sentence: "He knows that it is a terrible show." The word *although*, like other subordinating conjunctions, has the effect of turning an otherwise complete sentence into a fragment—good only for tacking onto another sentence. One way to correct this sort of error is to remove the subordinating conjunction:

> Danny wants to watch *Dynasty*. He knows that it is a terrible show.

Another way—and in this case probably a better representation of the author's intent—is to change the period at the end of the first sentence into a comma, thereby turning the two sentences into one:

> Danny wants to watch *Dynasty*, although he knows that it is a terrible show.

There are, of course, other grammatically correct ways of saying the same thing:

> Although Danny knows that *Dynasty* is a terrible show, he wants to watch it.

> Danny knows that *Dynasty* is a terrible show, but he wants to watch it anyway.

Fragments are not *always* incorrect, however. It's all right to use a fragment if (a) you *know* you're using it and (b) you know *why* you're using it. And why would you want to use a fragment? To create emphasis. Unless you're writing dialogue ("Hi. New car?"), that's really the only defensible reason for using a fragment. Here's an acceptable use of a fragment for the sake of emphasis:

> The other day my English professor spent half an hour complaining that television is moronic, that it wastes time that could be better spent, and that it has turned Americans from creative thinkers into hypnotized dummies. So when I dropped by his office that evening, what do you think he was doing? Watching *Dynasty*.

The third "sentence" in this passage lacks both a subject and a verb, and is therefore a fragment. A "corrected" version would read as follows:

> He was watching *Dynasty*.

But "correcting" the fragment weakens the effectiveness of the original. The emphasis is lost.

Fragments, then, can be useful. If you make deliberate use of them, however, you should do so sparingly; using too many fragments dissipates their effectiveness and can irritate, distract, and confuse your readers. Furthermore, since fragments are a rather sophisticated stylistic device, you should use them only when you are certain that they'll achieve the desired effect. The last thing you want is for your readers to think you made a mistake. So if you decide to use fragments intentionally, do so with good reason and choose your occasions with special care.

One closing question: where in this section have *I* used a fragment?

◆

Don't use sentence fragments unless you have good reason to do so.

14

*Every phrase and every sentence
is an end and a beginning.*
—T.S. Eliot, *Little Gidding*

♦

Comma Splices and Fused Sentences

A **comma splice** is a common punctuation error whereby two sentences are separated by a comma instead of a period. For instance:

> Henry VIII had six wives, he had two of them executed.

The simplest way to correct this error is to replace the comma with a period:

> Henry VIII had six wives. He had two of them executed.

There are alternatives, however. You can separate the two clauses with a semicolon:

> Henry VIII had six wives; he had two of them executed.

Or you can separate them with a coordinating conjunction:

> Henry VIII had six wives, and he had two of them executed.

You can subordinate one clause to another:

> Henry VIII had six wives, of whom he had two executed.

Or you can turn one clause into a phrase.

> Of his six wives, Henry VIII had two executed.

A similar error is the fused sentence. This is a case where two sentences—sentences that should have been separated by a period—have been placed end-to-end without anything in between:

> Nina bought a painting of a Campbell's Soup can last week it cost thirty thousand dollars.

Fused sentences may be corrected in much the same way as comma splices. The simplest solution is to put in the missing period:

> Nina bought a painting of a Campbell's Soup can last week. It cost thirty thousand dollars.

Or you may use a semicolon:

> Nina bought a painting of a Campbell's Soup can last week; it cost thirty thousand dollars.

Or you may add a coordinating conjunction:

> Nina bought a painting of a Campbell's Soup can last week, and it cost thirty thousand dollars.

Or you can subordinate one clause to the other:

> Last week Nina bought a painting of a Campbell's Soup can, which cost thirty thousand dollars.

Or, of course, you can rewrite the sentence entirely:

> Nina spent thirty thousand dollars last week on a painting of a Campbell's Soup can.

◆

Use appropriate punctuation to separate sentences.

15

We should agree as angels do above.
—Edmund Waller, *On Divine Love*

◆

Subject-Verb Agreement

A verb should **agree in number** with its subject. This is just another way of saying that if the subject is singular, the verb should be singular; if the subject is plural, the verb should be plural. For most writers, this rule is usually an easy one to remember; as long as the subject noun or pronoun and its verb are adjacent to each other, errors tend not to crop up. An error like the following, for instance, is rare:

> The photograph are on the mantelpiece.

But when the subject noun and its verb are separated by other words, it is easier for writers to slip up, as the following sentence demonstrates:

> The photograph of Whitney's three sisters
> are on the mantelpiece.

Here the verb *to be* is adjacent to the noun *sisters*; the writer, accordingly, has made the verb plural—*are*—so that it agrees with the plural noun *sisters*. But this is a mistake. Since it is the photograph that is on the mantelpiece (not the three sisters), the subject of this sentence is not the plural noun *sisters* but the singular noun *photograph*. The verb *to be* should therefore also be in the singular case—*is*, not *are:*

> The photograph of Whitney's three sisters is
> on the mantelpiece.

If you are a beginning writer who tends to make mistakes in subject-verb agreement, it's a good idea to read through everything you write just to check for agreement errors. Look for every verb, find its subject, and make sure that they match. Remember that in English most plural nouns have an *s* at the end; but with verbs the opposite is generally true—third-person, singular, present-tense verbs usually end in an *s* and plural, present-tense verbs usually don't:

Singular	The baby crie*s*. (verb ends in *s*)
Plural	The babie*s* cry. (noun ends in *s*)

Don't be fooled by sentences in which the word order is unusual—in which the subject, in other words, follows the verb. Consider the following sentence:

> Down the dark streets run the frightened, hungry boy.

The verb here is *run*. What is the subject? If you have any doubt, simply ask yourself: Who is doing the running? Not the streets, certainly. The answer, of course, is the boy. Therefore the subject is *boy*—a singular noun. And therefore the verb should be singular as well—not *run*, but *runs*.

> Down the dark streets runs the frightened, hungry boy.

The easy way to avoid being tripped up by a sentence like this is to imagine it with the words in their conventional order—subject followed by verb:

> The frightened, hungry boy runs down the dark streets.

The correct form of the verb here is clearly *runs*, not *run*. And no matter what the word order, as long as the subject remains the same, the verb should remain in the same form.

You don't need a plural noun to have a plural subject. Two or more singular nouns connected by the word *and* qualify as a plural subject:

> Los Angeles and San Diego are the two largest cities in California.

There are a few logical exceptions to this rule. When two connected nouns refer to a single person, place, thing, or concept, then the verb should be singular:

> "Oh, look, the lord and master is home," said Mrs. Estevez sarcastically as her husband entered the kitchen.

Here, "lord and master" is obviously a phrase that refers to a single individual, and so it takes a singular verb.

A singular verb is called for as well when two or more nouns, connected by the word *and*, are preceded by the word *each* or *every*. For instance:

> Every Tom, Dick, and Harry in town is in line to see this movie.
>
> Each boy and girl in my class has a driver's license.

But when the word *each* follows a series of two or more nouns connected by the word *and*, the verb should be plural:

> Jennifer and Lu-Ann each want to go to this movie.

When two or more singular nouns are connected by the word *or* or *nor*, the verb should be singular:

> Every week, when we go to the movies, either Jennifer or Lu-Ann picks up the tickets ahead of time.
>
> This week, however, neither Jennifer nor Lu-Ann was able to make it to the theater in time.

Similarly, if both nouns are plural, the verb should of course be plural:

> Neither the orchestra seats nor the balcony seats are comfortable.

The trouble arises when the subject consists of both singular and plural nouns. When this is the case, the verb should agree with the noun that is closest to it. Thus, in the following sentence, the verb *were* quite properly agrees with the plural noun *trailers:*

> When we went last week, neither the feature film nor the seven promotional trailers were interesting.

The same sentence would be equally correct as follows—with *was* in agreement with the singular noun *film:*

> When we went last week, neither the seven promotional trailers nor the feature film was interesting.

Since both are correct, which way to write it? In such a case, the deciding factor must be a stylistic one. Which one *sounds* better? Or do both versions, even though grammatically correct, sound awkward? If you decide that they do, you might want to rewrite the sentence entirely to avoid both the agreement problem and the awkwardness. Something like this might be better, for instance:

> We saw seven promotional trailers and a feature film last week, and none of them was interesting.

This version is both correct and stylistically pleasing—or at least not unpleasing. Note that the word *none* here takes a singular verb. This is because *none* is an "indefinite pronoun"—a pronoun that doesn't refer to any specific person, place, thing, or concept. The majority of indefinite pronouns—the most common of which include *anybody, anyone, anything, everybody, everything, nobody, no one, none, one, somebody, something*—take singular verbs when they function as subjects:

> Everybody loves somebody sometime.
>
> Something in the way she moves attracts me.
>
> Nobody is going to rain on my parade.

The rules of grammar tell us that singular nouns that refer to a group—such as *faculty, club, team*—may take either a singular or a plural verb, depending on whether the sentence in question refers to the group as a unit or as a number of separate individuals. Such nouns are called "collective nouns," and frequently they call for a singular verb, as in this sentence:

> The school orchestra is practicing its Billy Joel medley for the spring concert.

The rules tell us, however, that in a sentence such as the following, a plural verb is better:

> The school orchestra have been arguing a great deal about the merits of the Billy Joel medley.

Clearly, the plural verb makes sense here. An orchestra can *practice* as a unit, but when it *argues* it is not a unit at all but a number of individuals exchanging words with one another. Yet despite this logic, and despite the fact that the rules of English grammar say it's perfectly correct, it doesn't sound right. Indeed, the plural verb often sounds extremely awkward with a singular noun. What are we to do? We don't want to break the rule and we don't want to sound awkward either. The best thing to do, then, is to rewrite the sentence so that *orchestra* is no longer the subject. This is easily done:

> The members of the school orchestra have
> been arguing a great deal about the merits
> of the Billy Joel medley.

This way the subject of the sentence, *members*, is plural; the verb, *have been arguing*, is also plural; the sentence is both grammatically correct and stylistically inoffensive.

Often the word *number* can lead to agreement problems. Consider this sentence:

> A number of my friends is active in the pro-
> life movement.

Grammatically, *is* would seem to be the correct verb form here. After all, *number*—a singular noun—is the subject of the sentence, and the verb should agree with it. But the sentence *sounds* completely wrong. It sounds much better, in fact, with *are:*

> A number of my friends are active in the pro-
> life movement.

In such a case, I believe *are* should be preferred over *is*. Perhaps the best idea, however, would be to rewrite the sentence and avoid the problem altogether:

> Several of my friends are active in the pro-
> life movement.

There is another type of sentence that can cause confusion. It is the sort of sentence that contains a **linking verb**—a verb that connects a subject and a complement that both allude to the same person, place, thing, or concept. In the following sentence, *is* is a linking verb; note that the words *James* (the subject) and *my older brother* (the complement) both refer to the same person:

> James is my older brother.

One characteristic of simple sentences with linking verbs is that the subject and complement can be interchanged and the meaning will stay the same:

> My older brother is James.

This sentence poses no agreement problems. But what about the following sentence?

> My older brother's favorite rock group is the Rolling Stones.

Here, the subject, *rock group*, is singular; the complement, *the Rolling Stones*, is plural. Many beginning writers might make the mistake of having the verb agree with the complement, so that the sentence read as follows:

> My older brother's favorite rock group are the Rolling Stones.

Don't do this. The verb should agree with the subject, not the complement. If the subject and complement of this sentence were reversed, the verb would have to be changed accordingly, so that it agreed with the new subject:

> The Rolling Stones are my older brother's favorite rock group.

When it comes to agreement rules, titles are a special case. It doesn't matter whether a title "sounds" singular or plural; titles are always singular:

> *Cats* is, in my opinion, the best musical of the decade.

Similarly, when you refer to a word *as a word*, then it is also singular:

> *Women* is written on the door in imposing Gothic letters.

Don't be fooled by words like *news* that look plural, but are actually singular:

> "The news from Beirut is pretty grim," said Oscar.

And don't be fooled, either, by words like *media* and *data* that look singular, but are actually plural:

> "The news media are concentrating too much on the bad news," said Felix.

In spite of all these rules, there are times when the decision whether to make a verb singular or plural must depend on the context. For example, when the subject of a sentence is a word like *all* or *some*, the form of the verb must be discerned from the meaning of the sentence:

> "All of the money in this mattress is mine,"
> said Lucinda.

The subject noun of this sentence is *all*; it refers to money, a singular noun, and therefore the verb should be *is*. But the following sentence is different:

> "All of us are going to share equally," insisted Tatiana.

Here, *all* refers to *us*—a plural pronoun—and so the verb is plural: *are going*.

◆

Make certain that every verb agrees in number with its subject.

16

*Man . . . remembreth in them
Antecedence and Consequence.*
—Thomas Hobbes, *Leviathan*

♦

Pronoun-Antecedent Agreement

An **antecedent** is the word, phrase, or clause (usually a noun) to which a pronoun refers. Just as subjects must "agree" with their verbs, so pronouns must agree with their antecedents. And they must agree in three ways: in number, in gender, and in person. **Agreeing in number** means that if the antecedent is singular (*boy*), the pronoun should be singular (*he*); if the antecedent is plural (*boys*), the pronoun should be plural (*they*). **Agreeing in gender** means that a masculine antecedent (*boy*) takes a masculine pronoun (*he*), a feminine antecedent (*girl*) takes a feminine pronoun (*she*), a neutral antecedent (*house*) takes a neutral pronoun (*it*). **Agreeing in person** means that an antecedent in the third person takes a pronoun in the third person—and so forth.

The pronouns break down in this way:

First-Person Singular	I, me, my, mine, myself
First-Person Plural	we, us, our, ours, ourselves
Second-Person Singular	you, your, yours, yourself
Second-Person Plural	you, your, yours, yourselves
Third-Person Singular	he, she, it, his, her, hers, its, himself, herself, itself
Third-Person Plural	they, them, their, theirs, themselves

If you examine the preceding list carefully, you will see immediately why the following sentence is wrong:

> If one wishes to understand Woody Allen's movies, you should make a careful study of his essays.

In this sentence, "one," which is itself a pronoun, is intended to be the antecedent of the pronoun "you." But this is grammatically incorrect, because the two words don't agree in person: "one" is in the third person and "you" is in the second person. The sentence should be rewritten in either of the following ways:

> If you wish to understand Woody Allen's films, you should make a careful study of his essays.
>
> If one wishes to understand Woody Allen's films, one should make a careful study of his essays.

Similarly, the following sentence is grammatically incorrect:

> Brazil is an interesting country; they have a capital city in the middle of the jungle.

Here, "they" is intended to refer to "Brazil"; but, of course, "Brazil" is singular, so the pronoun must be "it":

> Brazil is an interesting country; it has a capital city in the middle of the jungle.

What about this sentence?

> Brian, David, and Rob arrived at the theater, and Brad gave each of them their tickets.

There are three pronouns in this sentence: *each, us* and *their*. The problem is with their, the possessive pronoun in the first-person plural. Its antecedent is *each*—which is not plural but singular. *Their* is therefore a mistake; the pronoun that is called for here—because it is the one that is consistent with *each*, and because all the persons named are male/masculine—is the third-person singular possessive pronoun, *his:*

> Brian, David, and Rob arrived at the theater,
> and Brad gave each of them his ticket.

But now that we've corrected it, there's a new problem with the sentence: *his* is ambiguous. *His* refers back to *each*, but it sounds as if it might refer to *Brad*—in other words, it sounds as if Brad is giving his own ticket away. This is a common pronoun problem, and one way to fix it is to eliminate *each* (which is not really a necessary pronoun here anyway), so that we don't have all these singular nouns and pronouns confusing us:

> Brian, David and Rob arrived at the theater,
> and Brad gave them their tickets.

◆

*Make certain that every pronoun
agrees in number with its
antecedent.*

III

Punctuation

17

No levell'd malice / Infects one comma in the course I hold.
—William Shakespeare, *Timon of Athens*

♦

Commas

Some teachers of writing are fond of saying that comma placement is easy: Wherever you'd pause for breath, just put a comma. I'm uncomfortable with this rule because it's not quite foolproof. In some cases it works, and in some cases it doesn't. Besides, it obscures the real purpose of commas. Commas do not exist in order to indicate pauses for breath. They exist, rather, to indicate grammatical relationships.

Look, for example, at the commas in the opening paragraph. Each is there for a reason. Take the first comma, for instance:

> Wherever you'd pause for breath, just put a comma.

As this excerpt illustrates, commas should be used after *most* introductory clauses or phrases—after word clusters, that is, which precede the main clause of a sentence. If you believe that an introductory clause or phrase is brief enough, and if omission of the comma does not create confusion, then you may omit the comma. Remember, too, that if a subordinate clause or phrase *follows* rather than precedes the main clause of the sentence, you don't need a comma. For example, if the clauses in the sentence "Wherever you'd pause for breath, just use a comma," were reversed, using a comma would be less acceptable:

> Just put a comma, wherever you'd pause for breath.

The next sentence of the opening paragraph, coincidentally, provides another example of a subordinate clause that follows the main clause:

> I'm uncomfortable with this rule because it's not quite foolproof.

Again, because the subordinate clause follows the main clause, we don't need a comma. (This is not to say that it would be wrong to use one.) If the clauses were reversed, however, a comma would be necessary:

> Because it's not quite foolproof, I'm uncomfortable with this rule.

Let's consider the next sentence of the opening paragraph—and the next comma rule:

> In some cases it's true, and in some cases it's not.

Here we have two main clauses, connected by the conjunction *and*. When you have two main clauses linked by a coordinating conjunction—*and, but, for, nor, or, so, yet*—a comma should probably precede the conjunction. Here again, though, the same exception applies: if the clauses are both brief enough, and if there is little possibility of confusion, you may omit the comma. No one, in other words, could justifiably fault you for writing:

> In some cases it's true and in some cases it's not.

The next sentence of the opening paragraph—

> Besides, it obscures the real purpose of commas.

—illustrates another rule: commas should be used after introductory transitional expressions. (Besides

besides, the list of transitional expressions includes *also, for example, for instance, in fact, indeed, moreover, nevertheless, on the one hand, on the other hand, therefore,* among others.)

And the next sentence of the opening paragraph demonstrates yet another rule—that commas should be used to set off parenthetical elements within sentences:

> They exist, rather, to indicate grammatical relationships.

If the word *rather* were placed at the beginning of the sentence, rather than within the body, the rule would be the same: use a comma to set it off.

> Rather, they exist to indicate grammatical relationships.

The word *rather* is a parenthetical element in this sentence. What that means is that removal of the word *rather* would do no damage to the sentence's grammatical coherence or to its essential meaning. A parenthetical element, as you probably know, may take the form of a full-length **nonrestrictive** phrase or clause:

> Norman Mailer, who recently wrote a one-thousand-page novel about ancient Egypt, must be an unusual man.

In this example, *who recently wrote a one-thousand page novel about ancient Egypt* is a nonrestrictive clause. And what is a nonrestrictive clause or phrase? It is a set of words that, like the word *rather* in our previous example, may be removed from a sentence without changing the sentence's essential meaning—and which is therefore set off from the main body of the sentence by commas. (The same phrase or clause could also be set off by using dashes or parentheses. See Section 23.)

A **restrictive** clause or phrase, on the other hand, is one that is essential to the meaning of the sentence and should therefore *not* be set off with commas. Take the following sentence:

> Any writer, who would write a one-thousand-page novel about ancient Egypt, must be an unusual man.

The commas in this sentence are a mistake. The test is to look at the sentence with the parenthetical clause removed:

> Any writer must be an unusual man.

Does it mean fundamentally the same thing as the original sentence? Clearly not. The parenthetical clause is therefore essential to the sentence—and therefore takes *no commas:*

> Any writer who would write a one-thousand-page novel about ancient Egypt must be an unusual man.

A further use for commas is to separate the items in a series that contains three or more items:

> Among the most popular British rock groups are Tears for Fears, Frankie Goes to Hollywood, and Culture Club.

One exception to this rule is when the items themselves within a series already contain commas; to avoid confusion you should separate those items with semicolons instead:

> Among the most popular British rock groups are Tears for Fears, which recorded the song "Everybody Wants to Rule the World"; Frankie Goes to Hollywood, which took its name from an old newspaper headline about Frank Sinatra; and Culture Club, about which too much has already been said.

Remember, too, that a comma should not be used before the first item of a series. The following sentence is therefore incorrectly punctuated:

> Among the most popular British rock groups are, Tears for Fears, Frankie Goes to Hollywood, and Culture Club.

Likewise, a comma should **not** be used ==after the last item in a series==. The punctuation in the following sentence is thus faulty:

> George Michael, Annie Lennox, and Marilyn, are all British pop stars as well.

The way it should read is as follows:

> George Michael, Annie Lennox, and Marilyn are all British pop stars as well.

Commas should also be used to separate coordinate adjectives—adjectives, that is, which modify the same noun:

> What do you think of these brash, bizarre British acts?

Note that there is no comma between *bizarre* and *British*, even though both are adjectives that modify the word *acts*. The reason for this is that *British* is more closely tied to the noun it modifies than are the other two adjectives. When this is the case, the final adjective and noun are treated as if they were a unit—in this case, *British acts*—and the comma between the last two adjectives is omitted.

Commas should, though, be used to separate the names of city and state, city and country, and so forth:

> Philadelphia, Pennsylvania, is known as the city of brotherly love.

Note that commas are used both before and after the word *Pennsylvania*. If you have to give an entire address, you should use commas to separate the name of the person or firm from the street address, the address from the municipality, the municipality from the state or country; zip codes, however, are not separated by commas:

> When they put me in prison the first thing I did was write to Norman Mailer, c/o Random House, 201 E. 50th Street, New York, New York 10022.

Commas are also used to separate titles that follow names:

> Actually, I addressed the letter to "Norman Mailer, B.E.," because I know he has a degree in engineering.

And commas serve a similar function in dates:

> January 31, 1987, was his birthday, so I called him up to wish him a happy one.

Note that commas both precede and follow the year in the date. If you choose to use the British method, with the date preceding the month—31 January 1987—you don't have to use commas.

Commas should also be used before and after **speaker tags** such as *he said* and *she asked:*

> "You don't know me," I said, "but I'm a big fan of yours, and I want to wish you a happy birthday."

If the speaker tag interrupts a quotation at a point where, if it were not a quotation, some other punctuation would be called for, that other punctuation should follow the speaker tag:

> "I read your book, Mr. Mailer," I said. "Where do you get your ideas?"

Commas that follow quotations should, as the preceding sentence illustrates, be placed *inside* the quotation marks. Commas should not be used, of course, when a quotation ends with a question mark or exclamation point:

> "Where did you get my number?" he bellowed.

Perhaps the majority of comma errors, in student writing anyway, do not involve missing commas but misused commas. The most common such mistake may well be the use of a comma to separate the subject of a sentence from its verb:

> That book by Norman Mailer, weighs about five pounds.

The subject of this sentence is *book;* the verb is *is;* there is no reason for the comma to be there. Yet many student writers would put it there. Make no mistake: this is absolutely wrong. The sentence should read:

> That book by Norman Mailer weighs about five pounds.

If you find that you are prone to commit this error, the best plan is to read one extra time through everything you write just to check for it. Find the subject and verb in every sentence and make sure that if there is a comma between them, it is there for a reason. In the following instance, for example, the commas are justified:

> That book, which I bought at a garage sale, weighs about five pounds.

The commas here separate the subject (*book*) and its verb (*is*), but are acceptable because they have a legitimate function: to set off the parenthetical element *which I bought at a garage sale.*

A less common but equally undesirable error is the placement of a comma between the verb and its object:

> That book on the end table weighs, about five pounds.

Another error is the placement of a comma before a coordinating conjunction when it does not link two main clauses:

> The two books on the end table are Norman Mailer's *Ancient Evenings*, and Jerry Hall's autobiography.

In this example, the comma is wrong because the words that follow *and* do not constitute a main clause. In the following example, the comma is correct because the word *and* is followed by a main clause:

> The red-covered book on the end table is Norman Mailer's *Ancient Evenings*, and the one beside it is Jerry Hall's autobiography.

Another familiar error is the placement of a comma after a coordinating conjunction:

> The Norman Mailer book looks interesting, but, my friend Dave says he'd rather read about Jerry Hall.

Here the comma before *but* is, of course, correct; the comma after it, however, is incorrect. The sentence should be written as follows:

> The Norman Mailer book looks interesting,
> but my friend Dave says he'd rather read
> about Jerry Hall.

You may also use commas to set off contrasting phrases. The last two sentences of the opening paragraph of this chapter, for instance, might instead have been combined into the following single sentence:

> Commas show grammatical relationships,
> not pauses for breath.

Though the words "not pauses for breath" do not constitute a main clause and therefore should not ordinarily be set off by a comma, in this case they do constitute a phrase that is set in contrast to the main clause, and therefore may take a comma.

Besides the bit about pausing for breath, there's another thing that composition teachers are fond of saying about the comma: "When in doubt, leave it out." Admittedly, it's a better rule than "Let your breath be your guide"—because the main problem most beginning writers have with commas is that they overuse them. If you follow this suggestion, then, chances are you will be correct more often than not. But an even better rule is "Don't *be* in doubt."

◆

Use commas thoughtfully.

18

At a comma, stop a little. . . . At a semicolon, somewhat more.
—Richard Hodges, *English Primrose*

◆

Semicolons

The **semicolon** has two main functions. Sometimes it serves the same purpose as a period—to separate two independent clauses that are not connected by *and*, *but*, or some other conjunction. Take the following two sentences, for example:

> Laaren's favorite song is "Material Girl" by Madonna. Lenny's is "Erlkoenig" by Franz Schubert.

If you wanted to, you could combine these two sentences:

> Laaren's favorite song is "Material Girl" by Madonna; Lenny's is "Erlkoenig" by Franz Schubert.

Why, you ask, would you *want* to use a semicolon instead of a period? It's a matter of style. Some writers like to use the semicolon to separate two independent clauses when the clauses enjoy a particularly strong relationship—when they are, in other words, closer in meaning or purpose than a run-of-the-mill pair of end-to-end sentences. That is clearly the case with the two sentences in the preceding example. Other writers do their best to avoid using semicolons at all for this purpose, and stick with the straightforward, elegant period. My own feeling is that, while overuse of the semicolon can result in singsong, irritating prose, a judicious use of the device now and then can be effective. In the preceding example, for instance, I think the version with the semicolon is definitely the better one; though both clauses are, grammatically speaking, independent clauses, they depend heavily upon each other.

A semicolon may also be used to separate more complicated units of words. Any two clusters of words that form grammatically complete sentences—whether simple, compound, complex, or compound-complex—may be separated by a semicolon. Look, for instance, at the last sentence in the previous paragraph.

In fact, you can even use a semicolon when the second independent clause begins with a coordinating conjunction like *and, but, or,* or *nor.* Take this sentence:

> Lenny is willing to listen to Laaren's Madonna record, but Laaren always pulls out the plug when Lenny puts on his Schubert LP.

Here the two clauses are connected by a comma; but if you wanted to use a semicolon, you'd be permitted to do so:

> Lenny is willing to listen to Laaren's Madonna record; but Laaren always pulls out the plug when Lenny puts on his Schubert LP.

Again, it's a question of style. A semicolon in this case would indicate a slightly longer pause between clauses. The net effect would be to give more individual emphasis to each of the two clauses. Of course, since there's nothing wrong with beginning a sentence with a coordinating conjunction, you could even use a period here, if you wanted to:

> Lenny is willing to listen to Laaren's Madonna record. But Laaren always pulls out the plug when Lenny puts on his Schubert LP.

Once more, it's a stylistic decision. To my ears, though, the period is a bit too strong a break in this particular case; I'd probably go with either the comma or the semicolon. How would I decide which? The decision would depend, to a large extent, on the surrounding text. If this reference to Lenny and Laaren came up in the course of an essay that was already too full of semicolons, I'd probably just use a comma. And if the essay had too many independent clauses connected by *and* or *but*, I would rewrite the excerpt to avoid monotony:

> Whereas Lenny is perfectly willing to listen to Laaren's Madonna record, Laaren always pulls the plug out when he puts on his Schubert LP.

The first function of the semicolon, then, is as an optional substitute for the period. Its second function is as a substitute for the comma—in *one* very specific situation. What situation? The listing of series of items. When you have such a series, and one or more of the items contains a comma, then instead of separating the items with commas, separate them with semicolons:

> The great American novelists of the nineteenth century are Nathaniel Hawthorne, author of *The Scarlet Letter*; Herman Melville, author of *Moby-Dick*; Mark Twain, author of *The Adventures of Huckleberry Finn*; and Henry James, author of *The Portrait of a Lady*.

Most mistakes that involve semicolons occur when a writer uses them in place of commas. For example, many beginning writers mistakenly use semicolons to separate independent clauses from subordinate clauses:

> Though Lenny is willing to listen to Madonna; Laaren refuses to listen to his German *lieder.*

The semicolon in this example should be a comma. Many mistakes, conversely, result from the use of commas when semicolons should be used:

> Lenny is willing to listen to Madonna, even so, Laaren refuses to listen to his German *lieder.*

The first comma here should be a semicolon:

> Lenny is willing to listen to Madonna; even so, Laaren refuses to listen to his German *lieder.*

Finally, sometimes semicolons are used mistakenly in place of colons:

> There are three things about Lenny that irritate Laaren; his fascination with classical music, his love of fine literature, and his refusal to keep in touch with his parole officer.

The semicolon here should be a colon. If you don't know why it should be a colon, stay tuned.

◆

Use the semicolon to separate two independent clauses that enjoy a close logical relationship.

19

Bursting out into wild accusing apostrophes to God and destiny.
—George Eliot, *Adam Bede*

◆

Apostrophes

The **apostrophe** has two major uses. One is to show possession:

> Is that Inez's new car over there, with the fur-covered dice hanging from the rearview mirror?

When you add *'s* to a word, make sure you are adding it to the right word. Don't, in other words, write anything like this:

> Is that the girl who went to school with you's car?

The *'s* in this sentence—if it belongs anywhere—belongs with the word *girl*, not with the word *you*. Since the construction of the sentence makes this impossible, it is necessary to rewrite the sentence entirely to make it grammatically correct. Here's one solution:

> Does that car belong to the girl who went to school with you?

If a plural noun ends in *s*, you need add only the apostrophe to create the possessive form:

> The students' cars are all parked behind the school.

If a plural noun doesn't end in *s*, though, the noun must be followed by *'s*, exactly as if it were a singular noun. When you write a plural possessive of this sort, make sure you put the apostrophe in the right place. One of the most common apostrophe errors among beginning writers occurs when, confronted with such a situation, they put the apostrophe *after* the possessive *s*. Here's an example of this kind of error:

The mens' gym is down the hall.

Here the plural noun is *men*, so the possessive should be *men's*. But the habit of putting apostrophes after the *s* when writing possessive plural nouns has caused the writer of this sentence to write *mens'*.

There is another common problem that arises from the habit of placing a single apostrophe after the plural *s*. Many beginning writers, when confronted by a singular noun that ends in *s*, will automatically add an apostrophe to create the plural—as if they were dealing not with a singular noun but with a plural noun:

> The school chorus' best number was "The Battle Hymn of the Republic."

Although this is permitted, the better practice is to add the *'s*. The word *chorus* is singular, so the possessive should take *'s:*

> The school chorus's best number was "The Battle Hymn of the Republic."

Not *all* possessives are indicated by the use of the apostrophe. The personal pronouns *my, mine, your, yours, his, her, hers, its, our, ours, their, theirs* require no apostrophe. Both of the following sentences are grammatically incorrect; removing the apostrophes would make them correct:

Punctuation

> Are all those records your's?
>
> I like your stereo, but our's has better sound quality.

The other major use of the apostrophe is to indicate omissions of letters in the usual contractions—words like *don't*, *won't*, *can't*, *we're*, *we'll*. Some teachers of composition frown on the use of contractions in formal writing; some professional writers, though, use them frequently. The best advice in this case is to know your audience.

By far, the most common apostrophe error of all involves the confusion over *it's*, *its*, and *its'*. If you have ever gotten this wrong, read this carefully and remember it: *it's* is a contraction meaning *it is*. (The apostrophe indicates the omission of the letter *i* in *is*.) For example:

> It's all right with me.
>
> It's your move.

Its is a possessive—a possessive *without* an apostrophe, which is no doubt what helps throw many beginning writers off—meaning *belonging to it*. Therefore:

> This record is missing its jacket.
>
> The best thing about your car is its fur-covered dice.

As for *its'*, there is no such word in English. Repeat: no such word. Nonetheless, many a confused writer uses it in place of *it's* or *its*. It's not correct in either circumstance.

Another common error is the confusion of *who's* and *whose*. *Who's* is a contraction for *who is:*

> Who's going to wash the car?

Whose is the possessive form of the word *who:*

> Whose job is it to wash the car?

Yet another familiar error is the use of apostrophes to indicate plurals. Apostrophes *never* indicate the plurals of words unless the words are referred to *as words:*

> I think I used too many *therefore*'s in that essay.

In such cases, the apostrophe is optional. The plural is equally acceptable without it:

> I think I used too many *therefore*s in that essay.

(Note that the *s* at the end of *therefore*, since it is not a part of the word-referred-to-as-a-word, is not italicized.)

The plurals of letters, numbers, symbols, and abbreviations *may* also take an apostrophe:

> He did not know where any of the YMCA's were in New York. (or YMCAs)

> There are two 8's in my social security number. (or 8s)

He's the only man I know with three Z's in his name. (or Zs)

The history of Europe in the 1930's does not make pleasant reading. (or 1930s)

Unbeknownst to me, the name of his company contained two &'s. (or &s)

◆

Use the apostrophe to indicate possessives and (in informal prose) contractions.

20

I quote others only in order the better to express myself.
—Michel de Montaigne, *Essays*

◆

Quotation Marks

Quotation marks—which most of us refer to in everyday conversation as "quotes"—have several uses. First, they are used to identify material that a writer has taken, word-for-word, directly from another source. For example, in an expository essay you might write something like this:

> Herman Melville's *Moby-Dick* begins with the famous and wonderfully simple line, "Call me Ishmael."

And a short story might begin as follows:

> Susan entered the kitchen and complained, "Out of paper towels again."

Remember, however, that indirect quotations—those that are *not* word-for-word—should *not* be placed within quotation marks. To write the following sentence in an essay on *Moby-Dick* would therefore be wrong:

> At the beginning of Melville's *Moby-Dick* the narrator tells us to "call him Ishmael."

One way to fix the sentence is simply to remove the quotation marks.

If a passage that you want to quote is more than four lines long, don't put it within quotation marks. Instead, indent it five spaces, *single spaced*. Many beginning writers, as if to be doubly safe, will mistakenly do both: that is, they will indent a passage *and* put it in quotation marks. This is wrong. Why? Because it is redundant—like wearing suspenders with a belt. The indentation itself indicates that the passage is a quotation; no further punctuation is necessary for the purpose.

What if you have to quote a passage that itself contains a quotation? Let's say, for example, that you want to quote the following sentence:

> The most significant line in modern American poetry is the third line of "The Love

> Song of J. Alfred Prufrock": "Like a patient
> etherised upon a table."

Since this quotation contains a quotation as well as a title in quotation marks, you must, in order to avoid confusing your reader, replace those quotation-marks-within-quotation-marks with *single quotation marks:*

> Professor Harris writes: "The most significant line in modern American poetry is the third line of 'The Love Song of J. Alfred Prufrock': 'Like a patient etherised upon a table.'"

As the preceding quotation demonstrates, a single quoted line of poetry may be run in with the text. But what if you want to quote more than one line of a poem? If the quotation is two lines long, you have a choice. You may, if you wish, quote the two lines in the course of the text as if they were prose, and indicate the line break with a slash (virgule):

> Hamlet expresses his suicidal melancholy in these unforgettable words: "Oh, that this too, too solid flesh would melt, / Thaw, and dissolve itself into a dew!"

Or, if you want to give the quotation greater prominence, you may indent it:

> Hamlet expresses his suicidal melancholy in these unforgettable words:
>
>> Oh, that this too, too solid flesh would melt,
>> Thaw, and dissolve itself into a dew!

If the quotation of poetry runs more than two lines, however, you should indent it, and reproduce the appearance of the poem on the page—its spaces, indentations, and so forth—as faithfully as possible:

> The first two stanzas of George Herbert's "Discipline" are representative, in style and tone, of a good deal of seventeenth-century religious poetry:
>
>> Throw away thy rod,
>> Throw away thy wrath:
>>   O my God,
>> Take the gentle path.
>
>>   For my heart's desire
>> Unto thine is bent:
>>   I aspire
>> To a full consent.

When writing dialogue, remember that every time you switch speakers, you should start a new paragraph—even if the lines of dialogue are only a sentence long.

> "Where are you from?" I asked.
> "Saskatchewan," she said.
> "Where's that?"
> "Canada."
> "That's north of here, isn't it?"
> She nodded. "How bright of you!" she said.
> I grinned modestly and explained, "I've always been into geography."

Note that commas are used to set off the speaker tags—that is, the *he said*s and *she said*s. If there is an exclamation point or question mark, however, where the comma should be, the comma is omitted. *Never* write anything like this:

> "Where are you from?", I asked.

When a quotation is more than one sentence long and is introduced by a speaker tag, it is better to use a colon than a comma:

> She told the police: "He keeps following me around. And he keeps asking all these questions. One question after another. And all about Canada."

Many beginning writers find themselves especially confused about punctuation when they use quotation marks. The rule is actually simple: place periods and commas *inside* quotation marks; place colons and semicolons *outside*. For instance:

> "Here," she said, "is that piece of sheet music you wanted."
> Taking it, I said, "Thank you"; but the song was "Hello Dolly": not the one I'd asked for.

As for question marks, exclamation points, and dashes, these punctuation marks should go *inside* quotation marks when they are part of the quotation or title, and should go *outside* when they are not. For instance:

> "Who," Stacy's mother demanded, "is that man who keeps calling you on the phone?"
>
> "His name is Felipe Francesco!" screamed Stacy. "And I love him!"
>
> Stacy's mother was in shock: Felipe Francesco was the name of the man who had published an article in the current issue of *Cosmopolitan* entitled "They Call Me Kinky"!
>
> "Is that the same man," she asked Stacy tearfully, "who wrote 'They Call Me Kinky'?"

If you have a question within a question, don't place two question marks together:

> Were you the one who asked "What's the capital of Missouri?"?

Instead, just keep the *internal* question mark:

> Were you the one who asked "What's the capital of Missouri?"

Or, better yet, rewrite the sentence so it doesn't contain a question within a question:

> Were you the one who asked what the capital of Missouri is?

Besides identifying quotations and spoken dialogue, quotation marks have a few other purposes. You should use them to mark the titles of shorter works and of a few other things—specifically, the titles of short stories, essays, articles, short poems, episodes of radio and television series, chapters of books, songs, music videos, unpublished dissertations, and courses and lectures. Some other titles, primarily those of longer works (books, magazines, and so forth), should be italicized or underlined. (See Section 25.)

Words referred to *as words* may be marked with either quotation marks or italics:

> Did you know that the word *chocolate* derives from a word in Nahuatl, the language of the Aztecs?
>
> The word "rhythm" looks as if it should have another vowel.

The only rule here is to be consistent. Don't switch back and forth between these two ways of marking words that are referred to as words. For the sake of clarity, choose one way and stick with it.

Many people are in the habit of using quotation marks to signify jargon, slang words, clichés, nicknames, and the like. In some cases this is good practice. Take the following sentence, for example:

> These short story writers are like soap opera writers, interminably obsessed with "relationships."

Here the word *relationships* has been put in quotation marks because the writer wants to make it clear that it is not the sort of word he or she would ordinarily use; it is, rather, the sort of word the short story writers under discussion would use—or at least it is the sort of word the writer of this sentence can imagine them using. This represents an acceptable use of quotation marks. So does this:

> I played cops-and-robbers with my nephew, and the game ended when he "shot" me.

Here, the word *shot* is put in quotation marks—and correctly so—because the writer is using the word facetiously: no one was really shot.

To use quotation marks to indicate a nickname, however, is unnecessary:

> Mary Lou came over last weekend with her husband, "Curly."

Granted, *Curly* may be an unusual name, but this is no reason to put it in quotation marks. That a word is slang or colloquial is not a good reason either:

> My seventh-grade teacher was a "dope."

The writer of this sentence clearly recognizes that the word *dope* is inappropriate diction for the piece of writing at hand. When this is the case, the solution is not to put the word in quotation marks but to exchange it for a more suitable word. Here's one alternative:

> My seventh-grade teacher was unintelligent.

Whenever you are tempted, then, to use quotation marks in an unorthodox situation—that is, when you are not actually quoting someone, writing dialogue, identifying a title, or referring to a word as a word—think carefully first. And, above all, use them sparingly.

◆

Mark quotations carefully.

21

*... I have seen them shiver and look pale, /
Make periods in the midst of sentences....*
—William Shakespeare, *A Midsummer
Night's Dream*

◆

Period, Question Mark, Exclamation Point

A **period** is used to end a declarative sentence:

> Elephants never forget.
>
> Diamonds are forever.

This includes declarative sentences in which questions have been incorporated:

> "Is it true that elephants never forget?" asked Jennifer.

Periods should also follow most abbreviations (see Section 27):

> Dr. Thompson walked into the classroom at exactly 1:00 p.m., carrying books by F. R. Leavis, T. S. Eliot, and W. E. B. DuBois.

Some abbreviations, including most acronyms—words like NATO and UNICEF, for instance, that are formed from the initials of words—do not take periods. And when a sentence ends in an abbreviation, do not add a second period:

> It took him only three years to earn his B.A.

Indirect questions—questions that the sentence under examination is merely telling us about—take a period:

> Jason asked me if I had ever worn a diamond.

Direct questions, on the other hand, take question marks:

> Have you ever worn a diamond?

When a direct question is included in a declarative sentence, the question mark should not be followed by a comma or period. The following sentences are punctuated incorrectly:

> "Have you ever worn a diamond?", Jason asked, pouring her a glass of champagne.
>
> She shook her head and asked, "Have you?".

The correct punctuation is as follows, with the question marks standing alone:

> "Have you ever worn a diamond?" Jason asked, pouring her a glass of champagne.
>
> She shook her head and asked, "Have you?"

A title that ends in a question mark, however, may be followed by a comma:

> After returning from class, I changed clothes, read "The Lady or the Tiger?", and had dinner.

Declarative sentences can be turned into questions:

> It took him only two years to earn his B.A.?

And, unlike periods, question marks can be used in a series, as follows:

> Have you ever worn a diamond? a ruby? a zircon?

The segments between the question marks may begin with lowercase letters, as above, or capitals:

> Have you ever worn a diamond? A ruby? A zircon?

The question mark may also be used within parentheses to indicate uncertainty about the correctness of a word, number, or date:

> The writer Sir Thomas Malory was born in 1405 (?).

An exclamation point is used to add emphasis to interjections, statements, and imperatives:

> "Wow! He gave you a diamond ring! Let me try it on!"

Don't overuse the exclamation point, however. It is the crudest way of achieving emphasis, and too many exclamation points remind one of dialogue in a comic book:

> Our trip to Washington, D.C., was so exciting! We toured the Capitol and the White House! We saw Barbara Bush walking her dog! Then we visited the Lincoln Monument! It was incredibly impressive!

In most cases, in fact, emphasis should be achieved by other means than by the use of exclamation points. Take the following sentence, for instance:

> Dr. Walters has performed 256 bypasses!

The writer of this sentence clearly wants to emphasize the statistic at the end of the sentence. Here are a couple of ways to do this without an exclamation point:

> Dr. Walters has performed no fewer than 256 bypasses.
>
> Dr. Walters has actually performed 256 bypasses.

◆

Use end punctuation precisely, making certain not to use periods and question marks together or to overuse exclamation points.

22

*Sleep! the Days Colon, Many Hours of
Bliss/Lost in a wide Parenthesis.*
—John Cleveland, *Poems Against Sleep*

◆

Colon

The **colon** is used to separate an independent clause (*preceding* the colon) from a set of words (*following* the colon) that the independent clause introduces. I use the expression "set of words" because what follows the colon may be any sort of grammatical unit. That unit may form a *full sentence* in its own right:

> There's one thing that bothers me about my apartment: the rats keep me up all night bumping into each other in the dark.

Or it may be a *phrase:*

> There's one thing that bothers me about my apartment: those rats scurrying around all night.

Or it may be just a *single word:*

> There's one thing that bothers me about my apartment: rats.

If the unit is a full sentence, you may—if you wish—begin it with a capital letter:

> There's one thing that bothers me about my apartment: The rats keep me up all night bumping into each other in the dark.

As these sentences demonstrate, the relationship between the independent clause preceding the colon and the set of words that follows the colon is often such that the *latter* explains or elaborates upon the *former.* One way of elaborating upon a statement is to provide a list, and a colon is particularly useful for this purpose—to separate, that is, a sentence from a list that it describes:

> I killed seven animals in my apartment yesterday: a rat, a cockroach, and five ants.

The preceding sentence is correctly written and punctuated. Many beginning writers, however, would mistakenly write something like the following:

> Yesterday, in my apartment, I killed: a rat, a cockroach, and five ants.

What's wrong with this sentence is that it doesn't *need* the colon. It should be written, therefore, as follows:

> Yesterday, in my apartment, I killed a rat, a cockroach, and five ants.

The colon may also be used to introduce a quotation:

> My rat problem reminds me of the remark by that famous philosopher: "I can solve the question of existence, but I don't know what to do about rats."

Usually when the words preceding the colon do not form an independent clause, it's best to introduce quotations not with a colon but with a comma:

> My rat problem reminds me of the famous philosopher who said, "I can solve the question of existence, but I don't know what to do about rats."

The colon has several other applications. It is used to set off a salutation in a business letter, to separate hours and minutes in the time of day, to separate chapter and verse in Bible references, to separate titles from subtitles, and to separate city and publisher in bibliographical references:

> Dear Mr. Sinatra:
>
> I was reading *Sinatra: An Unauthorized Biography* (New York: Macmillan, 1969) this morning at about 9:30 when I remembered the line from Proverbs 15:18: "A wrathful man stirreth up strife." Do you consider yourself a wrathful man?

◆

Use a colon to separate an independent clause from the set of words that it introduces.

23

In modern wit all printed trash is / Set off with num'rous breaks and dashes.
—Jonathan Swift, *Poems, On Poetry*

♦

Dashes, Parentheses, Brackets

Dashes, like commas, are used to set off parenthetical elements in the body of a sentence. Dashes or **parentheses** should be used instead of commas when the parenthetical element is an independent clause:

> Barbara wrote a fan letter to Sinatra—he's her favorite singer—but never got a reply.

> Barbara wrote a fan letter to Sinatra (he's her favorite singer) but never got a reply.

To avoid confusion, dashes or parentheses should also be used instead of commas when the parenthetical element itself contains commas:

> Barbara wrote a fan letter to Sinatra—her favorite singer, except for Madonna—but got no reply.

> Barbara wrote a fan letter to Sinatra (her favorite singer, except for Madonna) but got no reply.

There are other situations in which a parenthetical element would be confusing or ungrammatical if set off by commas. In these cases, too, either dashes or parentheses should be used.

> Barbara wrote a fan letter to Sinatra—who else?—but got no reply.

> Barbara wrote a fan letter to Sinatra (who else?) but got no reply.

To have used commas in the above sentence instead of dashes or parentheses would have been wrong, because a question mark cannot be followed by a comma:

> Barbara wrote a fan letter to Sinatra, who else?, but got no reply.

And to have used that parenthetical element *without* the question mark would have been confusing:

> Barbara wrote a fan letter to Sinatra, who else, but got no reply.

When proofreading your paper, make sure you've *closed* all parentheses and that, if you've set off a parenthetical element with a dash, you've ended it with another dash—unless the parenthetical element comes at the end of the sentence.

How do you decide whether to use commas, dashes, or parentheses to set off a parenthetical element? Here's a good rule: If you wish to lend emphasis to the parenthetical element, use *dashes;* if you wish to place less emphasis upon it, use *parentheses;* if you wish to give it approximately the same emphasis as the rest of the sentence, use *commas.*

Keep in mind, however, that excessive use of the dash—which is indicated in the typescript by two unspaced hyphens—is inadvisable; overuse blunts its effectiveness. You should know, too, that many teachers disapprove of the dash and will edit it out of any student paper in which they find it. Why? Probably because they have seen too many papers in which dashes are overused and some papers in which students (apparently uncertain of the correct rules of punctuation) have used the dash in place of *everything*—commas, periods, colons, semicolons, and so on. In reaction to the widespread use of this crutch, then, these teachers have declared war on the dash, even when it is used correctly. I, for one, think this is a shame. The dash is a fine punctuation mark and—when used wisely—can be elegant and effective.

A dash may also be used, like a colon, to separate an independent clause (preceding it) from a set of words (following it) that elaborate upon that clause. In all of the sentences in Section 22 that make use of the colon, the dash would have been perfectly acceptable instead:

> There's one thing that bothers me about my apartment—rats.

The choice between colon and dash, then, is largely a matter not of grammar but of individual style.

The dash is particularly useful when a word must be set off from its *appositive*—a word or phrase that defines or explains that word. Thus, in the following sentence a dash separates the word "nihilist" from its definition:

> Emma Goldman was a nihilist—an extreme revolutionary who believed in the destruction of the existing social order.

And the dash may be used to indicate a sudden breaking-off in conversation, usually due to an interruption:

> "Uh, oh," said Luke. "I pulled the pin out of the hand gren—"

Unlike dashes, parentheses may be used to enclose an entire sentence—in which case the period,

Dashes, Parentheses, Brackets   157

exclamation point, or question mark at the end of the sentence goes *inside* the parentheses:

> The real title of the Beatles' "white album" is, simply, *The Beatles.* (This was the first double album in recording history.)

If the parentheses enclose only part of a sentence, however, the period, exclamation point, or question mark should go *outside* the parentheses:

> The album *The Beatles* is popularly known as the "white album" (and was, incidentally, the first double album in recording history).

Parentheses can also be used to enclose the numbers and letters that mark the items in a list:

> The complaints he lodged against the motel were that (1) his pillow was lumpy, (2) there was no ice, (3) the television set received only the weather channel, and (4) there was a horse's head lying beside him when he woke up in the morning.

Avoid using numbers or letters in this manner except where clarity demands it. It's not grammatically wrong, just stylistically unattractive.

Brackets have a couple of important uses. They are used to set off words that you interpolate in a quotation from someone else—whether to comment, correct, or clarify:

> The famous songwriter wrote, "I owe everything to my idol, Gustav Mailer [Mahler], the great composer."

Brackets are also used in the place of parentheses-within-parentheses. But *don't* write any sentences that require you to do this. It should become necessary only in footnotes and bibliographies.

◆

> *Use dashes to set off parenthetical elements— especially when you want to emphasize those elements—but do so sparingly.*

24

Whistles low notes or seems to thrum his lute / As a mere hyphen 'twixt two syllables / Of any steadier man.
—George Eliot, *Spanish Gypsy*

♦

Virgules, Ellipses, Hyphens

The **virgule** (or **slash**) is used between words to indicate that both words are appropriate under the circumstances:

> I'm going to the opera tonight with Pamela and/or David.

This is, however, an ungainly and unattractive way to write. If it is possible to avoid using a virgule in this way, do so:

> I'm going to the opera tonight with Pamela or David, or perhaps with both.

The virgule is also used to separate lines of poetry that are not indented:

> One of Shakespeare's great soliloquies begins, "Oh, that this too, too solid flesh would melt, / Thaw, and dissolve itself into a dew."

The **ellipsis**—which consists of three spaced periods—is used to indicate that part of a sentence has been omitted from a quotation:

> Shakespeare wrote, "Oh, that this too, too solid flesh would . . . dissolve itself into a dew."

The ellipsis should *not* be used at the beginning of a quotation; and it should be used at the end of a quotation only to indicate that the quotation ends before the sentence ends:

> Shakespeare wrote, "Oh, that this too, too solid flesh would melt. . . . "

Note that the quotation ends with *four* periods. The first period is the *period*; the next three are the *ellipsis* that indicates the omission of the rest of the sentence.

Virgules, Ellipses, Hyphens 161

If a full sentence or more is omitted from a quotation, then there should also be four periods: one to indicate the termination of the sentence preceding the omission (unless, of course, this sentence ends in an exclamation point or question mark), and the next three to indicate the omitted sentence.

An ellipsis can also be used to indicate a pause in conversation:

"An . . . ellipsis? What's that?

Or to indicate the trailing-off of a statement:

"It . . . well, you wouldn't understand . . . "

Hyphens are used in certain compound words, notably those beginning with *all*, *ex*, and *self*. Be aware of this, and always check a dictionary if you're not sure whether a certain word is hyphenated or not.

Hyphens are also used between two or more words that serve as a compound adjective:

Did you see that blue-eyed girl?

When compound adjectives follow the noun that they modify, though, they are not hyphenated:

That girl is blue eyed.

Hyphens are also used in numbers from twenty-one to ninety-nine, including when they are part of larger numbers:

> The grocery bill came to one hundred and twenty-five dollars.

Hyphens are also used in fractions used as compound modifiers:

> Our dog Lucy is one-half collie and one-half Great Dane.

If a fraction does not modify anything, however, no hyphen should be used:

> I bought a pizza and gave Lucy one half.

Hyphens are also used to avoid ambiguity in words that, without hyphens, would be mistaken for other words:

> Suzy and I decided to re-form our club.

The hyphen here is used to prevent the word *re-form* (meaning "to form again") from looking like *reform* ("to correct").

Hyphens are also used when prefixes are added to the beginnings of capitalized words:

> Who is your favorite post-Impressionist artist?

◆

Don't use virgules, ellipses, and hyphens indiscriminately.

IV

Mechanics

25

*. . . before the invention of italics, stage
directions were often mistaken for dialogue,
and great actors frequently found
themselves saying, 'John rises, crosses left.'*
—Woody Allen, *Getting Even*

◆

Italics

Unless you happen to write on a word processor with a dot-matrix printer, you can't really put anything in **italics.** What you can do on any typewriter, however, is underline. Thus underlining has come to be accepted as the manuscript equivalent of printed italics.

But when do you use italics? There are actually several uses, none of which has anything to do with any of the others. Italics are a multipurpose device.

First, italics are used when a foreign word or phrase is included in an English sentence:

> A lot of these teenybopper movies nowadays consist of nothing but *rite de passage* sequences.

> Evelyn Waugh, writes Joseph Epstein, "possessed the gift of viewing everything as if from a great distance, *sub specie aeternitatis*—under the aspect, that is, of eternity, from which aspect nearly everything humankind does is of course ridiculous, absurd, comical."

> The family down the block, like any *nouveau riche* family, has gone and bought a Cadillac.

There's no clear line in these matters. Some foreign words are well on their way to being English words; with such words, the question is whether they are past the italicization stage. Check a good-sized English dictionary; if a word appears there, then italics are optional, if not unnecessary. *Amigo*, for example, is listed in my Webster's.

Why, then, did I italicize it in the previous sentence? Because I was referring to it *as a word*. I wasn't talking about an amigo, but about the word *amigo*. This is the second use for italics: to indicate words or letters that are referred to as such. (Quotation marks may also be used for this purpose. But be consistent: don't switch from one to the other within a single piece of writing.) For example:

> The word *crippled* sounded harsh, so many people dropped it and began using *handicapped*, which sounded nicer. In recent years, however, *handicapped* has also begun to sound harsh to many ears, so it has been widely replaced by *disabled*. But we are already seeing the beginning of the end of *disabled*, I think: I saw Ted Kennedy, Jr., on television the other day and he says he dislikes *disabled*, because the word implies that one is unable to do things. The designation he prefers is *physically challenged*.

Why did I italicize the words *as a word* in the preceding paragraph? Because I wanted to emphasize them. This is the third use for italics: to emphasize a word or phrase. It's a good stylistic device—when used sparingly. (If you use it *too* much, you *destroy* the effect and irritate *everybody*.) Here is an example of the proper use of italics for emphasis:

> "I knew I was a bastard," Truman Capote once wrote, "but forgave myself because I was *born* a bastard—a talented one whose sole obligation was to his talent."

But *caveat auctor* (that's Latin for "let the writer beware"). Student writers tend to overuse italics, because they are the *easiest* way of indicating where one wants the emphasis in a sentence to go. Remember that there are other, more sophisticated ways of dictating emphasis—for example, by shifting word order—and that in some cases these ways may well be preferable to the use of italics. In the sentence where I italicized *easiest*, the emphasis could probably be achieved more elegantly. Here's one way of rewriting it:

> Student writers tend to overuse italics because, of all the ways of indicating where the emphasis in a sentence should go, they are one of the easiest.

Thus, I've removed the italics from *easiest*, but by moving the word to the end of the sentence, I've managed to retain the emphasis on the word.

The fourth function of italics is to indicate titles. Everyone knows that italics and quotation marks are both used for this purpose. But when do you use one and when do you use the other? To many student writers the distinction seems very confusing. But it needn't be. The distinction is actually quite simple. Titles of *longer* works take italics; titles of *shorter* works take quotation marks.

Thus, the names of books, magazines, journals, newspapers, pamphlets, movies, plays, long poems, radio and television series, record albums, ballets, operas, long musical works, and videocassettes should be italicized. (The names of paintings, sculptures, ships, spaceships, trains, and airplanes are also italicized.) The names of short stories, essays, articles, short poems, episodes of radio and television series, chapters of books, songs, and music videos should be placed within quotation marks. (The same applies to the titles of unpublished dissertations—no matter how long the titles are—and courses and lectures.)

Many of these short works are of the sort that are usually incorporated in longer works. For example:

> Did you see Dana Gioia's poem, "In Chandler Country," in the *New Yorker* magazine?
>
> The best song in *Purple Rain* was "When Doves Cry."
>
> The last story in David Leavitt's book *Family Dancing* is called "Dedicated."
>
> The funniest episode of *The Mary Tyler Moore Show* is "The Death of Chuckles the Clown."
>
> One of the most famous arias is *"La Donna e Mobile"* from Verdi's *Rigoletto.* [I have italicized the title of the aria not because it is a title but because it is in Italian.]
>
> Nothing was on television, so I opened up the *Encyclopaedia Britannica* and read a fascinating article called "Sandflies."

There are some exceptions to these rules. The title of an instrumental work that isn't really a title at all but consists merely of the form and number (for example, Beethoven's Fifth Symphony) is neither italicized nor placed in quotation marks. The same applies to sacred religious writings (the Bible, the Book of Genesis, the New Testament, the Talmud, the Koran, and so forth) and the parts of a book that aren't really titles (Preface, Chapter One, Appendix, Index).

Though book publishers and scholarly and professional journals follow these standard rules of italicization strictly, many newspapers and popular magazines have devised their own variations on these rules. Don't be confused by this. There's usually a good reason. For instance, many newspapers do not have italic typefaces, so the editors place all titles in quotation marks.

There are gray areas, too. How long must a poem be to qualify as a "long poem"? Clearly, a sonnet of fourteen lines is a short poem, and a poem that runs a hundred or so pages is a long poem. But what about a poem like T. S. Eliot's *The Waste Land*, which contains 434 lines? I've chosen to think of it as a long poem—and have therefore italicized it—but I've seen its title printed both ways. The rules about where to draw the line between a long poem and a short poem aren't precise. When you face a problem like this, the important thing is to be consistent: draw your own line, and stick to it. By italicizing *The Waste Land*, I've made a commitment that applies to this entire book: if I mention any poem of 434 lines or more anywhere in these pages, I've got to italicize it, because I've italicized *The Waste Land*. Comprende?

◆

*Use italics to indicate the titles
of longer works.*

26

I love capitals.
—Lord Chesterfield, *Letters*

♦

Capitals

Proper names are capitalized. That includes the names of specific people, places, and things; specific nations, nationalities, religions, languages, historical events, documents, publications, movements, organizations, associations, institutions, college courses (but not subjects), brand names, months and days of the week, and so forth:

Thomas Jefferson
George Bernard Shaw
Florence, South Carolina
Southern California
the South [specific region], Southern, Southerners
France, Frenchmen, French
North America
Free Will Baptist Church, a Baptist
Bastille Day
Gettysburg Address
California State University, Northridge
Biology 101
American Medical Association
Windex

Nouns that do not indicate specific persons, places, things, and so forth, are not capitalized:

a medical association
a university
a church
a bottle of window cleaner
a course in biology
south [compass direction]
a southern exposure

Seasons (*winter, spring, summer, fall*) are not capitalized. But words that derive from proper names are routinely capitalized:

> Jeffersonian democracy
> French toast
> Carolina wren
> Marxism [from Karl Marx]
> Freudian [from Sigmund Freud]
> Shavian comedy [from George Bernard Shaw]

Abbreviations or acronyms formed from words that are usually capitalized are capitalized:

> G. B. S. [from George Bernard Shaw]
> S. C.
> NATO
> CSU, Northridge [from California State University]
> AMA [from American Medical Association]

And titles that precede a proper name are capitalized—but *only* when they precede the name:

> President Thomas Jefferson
> Doctor Sigmund Freud
> Professor Zimbardo
> Aunt Rose

> Sigmund Freud was a doctor.
> Here comes Zimbardo, the professor.
> Rose is my aunt.

Whether *President* (referring to the President of the United States) is capitalized when *not* preceding a proper name is a toss-up. Whatever you decide, just be consistent.

When writing the titles of books, movies, essays, and so forth, capitalize the first and last word of the title and all other words except articles (*a, an, the*), brief conjunctions (*and, but, or*), and prepositions (*in, of, to*). But even the shortest pronouns (*he, she, we, it*), verbs (*am, are, is*), nouns, adjectives, and adverbs *are* capitalized:

> *From Here to Eternity*
>
> *Why Are We in Vietnam?*
>
> *To Be or Not to Be*
>
> "Is You Is or Is You Ain't My Baby?"

The words *I* and *O* are always capitalized; *oh* is not, unless it begins a sentence.

The first word of every sentence is capitalized, as is the *first* word of a direct quotation:

> Stacey asked, "Who wrote *Zuckerman Unbound?*"
>
> "Don't you know," I said, "that it's Philip Roth?"
>
> "Don't you know?" I said. "It's Philip Roth."

Sentences in parentheses should be capitalized:

> Stacey asked a question about Philip Roth. (He happens to be my favorite writer.)

But don't confuse sentences in parentheses with parenthetical elements within other sentences:

> Stacey asked a question about Philip Roth (my favorite writer).

And short quoted phrases incorporated in sentences are *not* capitalized:

> Ed Rothstein described *Zuckerman Unbound* in *The New York Review of Books* as "affecting and intriguing."

◆

Capitalize the first word of every sentence and all proper names.

27

*But it is one Thing to Abbreviate
by Contracting, Another by
Cutting off.*
—Sir Francis Bacon, *Essays*

◆

Abbreviations

As a rule, most abbreviations are inappropriate in any type of writing above the level of the grocery list. You may be tempted, in particular, to abbreviate the names of continents (*Eur., N. Amer.*), countries (*W. Ger., Fr.*), states (*S.C., Mass.*), months (*Jan., Dec.*), days of the week (*Mon., Wed.*), units of measurement (*in., ft., cm.*), college courses or subjects (*Bio. 101, poli. sci., anthro.*), thoroughfares (*Coit St., Mad-*

ison Ave., Reseda Blvd., Long Island Expwy., Herald Sq.), rivers or mountains (*Mississippi R., Mt. McKinley*), or the parts of a book (*Vol. One, Chap. Two, Pg. 3*)—but resist the temptation. In the preceding examples, *all* the words should be spelled out.

There are exceptions, however. The United States may be referred to as the U.S.A. or the U.S., the Soviet Union as the U.S.S.R. The abbreviation *D.C.*, for District of Columbia, is permissible for *Washington, D.C.* There's nothing wrong with using familiar acronyms for corporations, agencies, organizations, and the like—for example, *ITT, CIA, NBC, KKK, NFL*. Abbreviations like *Inc.* and *Co.* may be used when they are actually part of a company's name. And units of measure commonly referred to by their abbreviated names, such as *rpm* (for *revolutions per minute*) are acceptable.

Some abbreviations are not only permitted but required by the rules of written English. Titles following proper names, for example, are abbreviated: *M.D., Ph.D., M.A., M.B.A., D.D.S., J.D., S.J., Sr., Jr.*, and so forth. Academic titles such as *Ph.D.* and *M.A.* may even be used apart from proper names, as the following sentence illustrates:

> At the rate things are going, by the year 1999 every man, woman, and child in America will have an M.B.A.

Aside from the titles that follow proper names, there are certain titles *preceding* proper names that should be abbreviated: *Mr., Mrs., Ms., Dr.,* and *St.* (for *Saint*). (Don't be redundant: either *Dr. Benjamin Spock* or

Benjamin Spock, M.D. is fine; but *Dr. Benjamin Spock, M.D.* is wrong.) Other titles are routinely abbreviated when used with a proper name—for example, *Rev.* for *Reverend*, *Prof.* for *Professor*, *Sen.* for *Senator*. But don't abbreviate any of these words when they're not being used in conjunction with proper names; in ordinary usage, that is, *spell out* the words *doctor, saint, reverend, senator,* and so forth.

Similarly, such abbreviations as *A.D. (anno Domini), B.C. (before Christ), C.E. (Christian era), A.M. (ante meridian), P.M. (post meridian), no. (number), PST (Pacific Standard Time)* may be used with specific dates, times, and numbers. Remember that *A.D.* should *precede* the year (A.D. 1986, not 1986 A.D.). The Latin-derived abbreviations *i.e. (id est,* meaning "that is"), *e.g. (exempli gratia,* meaning "for example"), *et al. (et alia,* meaning "and others"), *etc. (et cetera,* meaning "and so forth"), *N.B. (nota bene,* meaning "note well"), *v.* or *vs. (versus)* are acceptable but don't overuse them. For the most part—with the exception of the very common *i.e.* and *e.g.*—you should probably restrict the use of Latin-derived abbreviations to footnotes, bibliographies, and parentheses.

❖

Avoid most abbreviations except in the most informal pieces of writing.

28

the honor'd Number
—William Shakespeare,
Coriolanus

◆

Numbers

To spell out or not to spell out? That's the question, and the simplest answer is as follows. If the number can be written out in one or two words, then do so; if it requires more than two words, then use numerals. You would, therefore, spell out the number 500, because *five hundred* is only two words; but you would not spell out 499, because *four hundred and ninety-nine* is three words (a hyphenated number is considered one word).

An important exception to this rule is that when several numbers appear together, they should all be handled the same way. If you had to use *500* and *499* in the same sentence, for example, you would write them both in numerals. Another important exception is that you should *never* begin a sentence with numerals. The following sentence, therefore, is wrong:

> 499 people showed up for Allen Ginsberg's poetry reading.

The sentence should be rewritten as follows:

> Four hundred and ninety-nine people showed up for Allen Ginsberg's poetry reading.

There are always alternatives, of course. If you think the sentence looks unwieldy, or just kind of odd, with that number spelled out, you can always rewrite it:

> Allen Ginsberg's poetry reading drew a crowd of 499.

The other major exceptions to the rule are pretty commonsensical. Numerals may be used for dates (2 May 1959), addresses (9600 Reseda Boulevard, Apt. 237), decimals (3.14159), percentages (49.5%), fractions (2/7), ratios (2 to 1), statistics; for highway numbers (Route 25), television and radio stations (WNBC Radio, 66 AM), names of monarchs (Charles V), office numbers (Room 19), the designations of the various parts of literary works and other publications (Act I, Scene 2; Volume I, Chapter 2, page 425, line 66).

Commas should be used to separate three-digit groups in numbers containing four or more digits:

> Joey claimed that his father had $2,550,000 in the bank.

But this rule does not apply to house numbers, radio frequencies, or decimals. Nor does it apply to numbers on licenses or license plates, social security cards, credit cards, passports, identification cards, bank accounts, and the like. The omission of commas from four-digit numbers is an increasingly frequent occurrence.

◆

Spell out all numbers that require two or fewer words.

V

Stylistics

29

Style is the dress of thoughts.
—Lord Chesterfield, *Letters*

♦

Finding a Style

Developing as a writer is, to a large extent, a matter of finding your own **style.** Notice that I have said "finding" and not "creating." In writing, a style is not something that you consciously create. It is, rather, something that you attain gradually. You may begin playing baseball as a child and discover only after years of practice what position you are best suited for; similarly, you may spend years writing before you find yourself writing in your natural style. Like the clothes you wear, the style of your writing—when it is truly original and not thoughtlessly imitative—is the mirror of your personality. And that style need not be flashy or flamboyant; in fact, it should *not* be flashy or flamboyant, unless you yourself are flashy or flamboyant.

For style is, to put it simply, the rendering of your personality on paper. It is the fingerprint you leave on everything you write, whatever the subject may be; it is the mark that identifies your writing as uniquely yours. There are few things a teacher of writing responds to more enthusiastically than students with a firm sense of style—students who know what they think and feel and who have a distinctive and natural way of expressing those thoughts and feelings. And this is true not only of writing teachers but of all readers. To say that a piece of writing is marked by a distinctive style is to say that one has the sense of a *person* speaking—and a reader, any reader, is more likely to be interested in facts, stories, descriptions, arguments, when they seem to originate from a real person and not just from a piece of paper with words on it.

Many well-known writers are easily recognizable by their styles. John Updike (1932–   ), for instance, tends to write numerous descriptive passages, and his descriptions are usually precise and rich with elaborate and clever metaphors. The following sentences from the beginning of his story, "A Sense of Shelter," demonstrate these tendencies:

> Snow fell against the high school all day, wet big-flaked snow that did not accumulate well. Sharpening two pencils, William looked down on a parking lot that was a blackboard in reverse, car tires had cut smooth arcs of black into the white, and wherever a school bus had backed around it, it had left an autocratic signature of two V's. The snow, though at moments it whirled opaquely, could not quite bleach these scars away. The temperature must be exactly 32°. The window was open a crack, and a canted pane of glass lifted outdoor air into his face, coating the cedarwood scent of pencil shavings with the transparent odor of the wet window sill. With each revolution of the handle his knuckles came within a fraction of an inch of the tilted glass, and the faint chill this proximity breathed on them sharpened his already acute sense of shelter.

Henry James (1843–1916) was also a descriptive writer. But whereas Updike concentrates on surface details, James is most identifiable by his precise descriptions of characters' thoughts, as well as by his long, complex, and sometimes hard-to-follow sentences. As the following passage from his story "The Tree of Knowledge" illustrates, James's sentences are frequently interrupted by such modifying phrases as "to the best of his belief" and "last not least":

> It was one of the secret opinions, such as we all have, of Peter Branch that his main success in life would have consisted in his never having committed himself about the work, as it was called, of his friend Morgan Mallow. This was a subject on which it was, to the best of his belief, impossible with veracity to quote him, and it was nowhere on record that he had, in the connexion, on any occasion and in any embarrassment, either lied or spoken the truth. Such a triumph had its honour even for a man of other triumphs—a man who had reached fifty, who had escaped marriage, who had lived within his means, who had been in love with Mrs. Mallow for years without breathing it, and who, last not least, had judged himself once and for all.

Ernest Hemingway (1899–1962) was also a descriptive writer—but, unlike James, he avoids going into detail about his characters' thoughts, and, unlike Updike, he describes surface details with great simplicity, using few adjectives and adverbs and even fewer metaphors. He is famous for his simple sentences, for his deliberately limited vocabulary, for his short, effective lines of dialogue, and for the occasional multiple compound sentence that consists of a string of simple clauses connected by conjunctions. Here, for example, is the first paragraph of his famous story, "A Clean, Well-Lighted Place":

> It was late and every one had left the cafe except an old man who sat in the shadow the leaves of the tree made against the electric light. In the daytime the street was dusty, but at night the dew settled the dust and the old man liked to sit late because he was deaf and now at night it was quiet and he felt the difference. The two waiters inside the cafe knew that the old man was a little drunk, and while he was a good client they knew that if he became too drunk he would leave without paying, so they kept watch on him.

Toni Morrison (1931–) has what might be described as a middle style. Her prose is richly descriptive, deriving much of its impact from its touches of nature imagery and its matter-of-fact retailing of exotic names and eccentric incidents, but it is not as extravagant in its language or metaphors as Updike's. Morrison is concerned with her characters' thoughts, but does not delineate them as elaborately as James; her style is unadorned, but nowhere near as drastically simple as Hemingway's. The following excerpt from the opening paragraph of her short novel *Sula* provides a good example of a style that does not draw immediate attention to itself but is capable of achieving very impressive effects:

In that place, where they tore the nightshade and blackberry patches from their roots to make room for the Medallion City Golf Course, there was once a neighborhood. It stood in the hills above the valley town of Medallion and spread all the way to the river. It is called the suburbs now, but when black people lived there it was called the Bottom. One road, shaded by beeches, oaks, maples and chestnuts, connected it to the valley. The beeches are gone now, and so are the pear trees where children sat and yelled down through the blossoms to passersby. Generous funds have been allotted to level the stripped and faded buildings that clutter the road from Medallion up to the golf course. They are going to raze the Time and a Half Pool Hall, where feet in long tan shoes once pointed down from chair rungs. A steel ball will knock down Irene's Palace of Cosmetology, where women used to lean their heads back on sink trays and doze while Irene lathered Nu Nile into their hair. Men in khaki work clothes will pry loose the slats of Reba's Grill, where the owner cooked in her hat because she couldn't remember the ingredients without it.

Each of these three writers' styles could be described in far greater detail—as containing, for example, a certain proportion of nouns to verbs, of concrete nouns to abstract nouns, of active verbs to passive verbs, of words of Anglo-Saxon origin to words of Latin origin, and of simple sentences to complex sentences. Yet none of these writers sat down and said, "Hm, I'm going to use active verbs, Anglo-Saxon words, and concrete nouns." All attained their mature styles as the result of long periods of growth and gradual self-discovery. If they ended up writing more compound than complex sentences, or vice-versa, it was not because they made a rational choice between the two, but because the type of sentence they gravitated toward proved to be a more suitable medium for conveying their sense of themselves and their vision of the world. For instance, Hemingway developed his deceptively simple style only after having been influenced, over the course of several years, by a number of important writers in turn—among them, Mark Twain, Stephen Crane, Sherwood Anderson, and Gertrude Stein—as well as by the style sheet of the Kansas City *Star*, for which he had worked as a cub reporter.

Which brings us to the question of imitation. I have said that a writing style should not be "thoughtlessly imitative." But this is not to say that it should not be imitative at all. On the contrary, it's a good thing for beginning writers to take as their models the works of established writers that they admire. The secret is not to imitate one writer slavishly but to take what you need from that writer for your own purposes. Most beginning writers do this instinctively. They find a writer whose work they like, they read several of his or her books, and when they sit down to write they find themselves writing more like that writer than they did before. Sometimes this happens without the beginning writer even realizing it. For example, when I was a freshman in college, I read all of Kurt Vonnegut's novels and wrote several papers for my English composition course before I realized that their style owed a great deal to my reading of Vonnegut. As a matter of fact, they owed *too much* to Vonnegut: anyone reading them would have thought that I was trying to copy Vonnegut's style. After I'd read a few more books by different writers, though, and Vonnegut had faded a bit into the past, my papers came to sound less like Vonnegut. But some of the influence remained. My writing was sharper and simpler than it had been before I'd read Vonnegut; it was *better*—my teacher's reactions made that obvious—and it flowed from me more naturally and smoothly than it had before.

What had happened was that reading Vonnegut had helped me to move closer to my natural style—to approach a way of writing that would come to me more easily and that would express my personality with greater precision and fidelity than the way I had written beforehand. Another student who had read a few Vonnegut novels, but whose natural style did not lie in that direction, would never have absorbed Vonnegut's influence, because Vonnegut's work would not have struck him in the same way it struck me. After all, in the same year that I read these Vonnegut novels, I read books by several other writers, some of them better writers than Vonnegut—but I was never drawn, consciously or subconsciously, to

Finding a Style 193

imitate their style of writing. The reason was that my own natural style did not lie in those directions.

A good way to develop your own style, then, is to do a lot of reading. Be curious: if a book at the library or on a friend's bookshelf looks interesting, pick it up and read the first paragraph; you just may find a voice that speaks to you. Know what you like, and trust and follow your instincts. This, of course, is simply another way of saying "Know yourself." And it's true that the surer you are of who you are and what you believe, what you like and don't like, the better position you're in to establish an original style that reflects your tastes and attitudes. One thing that makes writing difficult for many student writers is that they simply don't have a firm sense of who they are as writers. A teacher will say, "Write about your summer vacation," and student writers without a firm sense of their identity as writers will be confused and lost. "What," they will wonder, "does the teacher expect of us?" Does the teacher want them to be serious or lighthearted, to cover one incident or the entire vacation, to describe the places they saw or relate the conversations they had, or to elaborate upon the bittersweet, thoughtful mood that summer has left behind? They will, in fact, be so preoccupied with wanting to be what the teacher expects them to be that they won't realize the teacher probably just wants them to be *themselves*—to write about whatever is most important to *them*, in whatever way comes most naturally (as long as it's grammatically correct).

And make no mistake: most English teachers—

and most readers in general—can tell when someone is speaking in his or her natural voice. They can tell, too, when someone is taking on a different voice—usually in an attempt to sound "impressive." This is one reason why it's a bad idea to use a fancy word that you're unfamiliar with: because more often than not, your readers will sense immediately that you're unfamiliar with the word. Such attempts to sound "impressive" are common among beginning writers. They're insecure; they think their own thoughts, ideas, and experiences are not worth any reader's attention. So they try, on paper, to be someone else—usually someone with a bigger vocabulary, deeper thoughts, loftier ideas, and a vaster experience of the world. For a writer to behave in this manner is simply self-destructive. So try to avoid it. When you sit down to write, don't try to be whatever you think your teacher wants you to be—a studious and ambitious young conservative, a righteous and sensitive liberal, or what-have-you—but try, as well as you can, to be yourself. Speak your own thoughts and feelings in your own voice—or as close as you can come to it. For to an English teacher, students who are not out to please or to pretend, but who are truly endeavoring to discover themselves as writers, are a joy forever.

◆

When you write, be yourself.

30

But it is better to fail in originality than to succeed in imitation.
—Herman Melville, quoted in *The Literary World*

◆

Clichés

A **cliché** is a set of words that has been used so many times, by so many writers, that it is worn out beyond the point of usefulness. That is to say, readers have seen the same combination of words so often that the words no longer succeed in evoking the idea or image that they originally did. Look at it this way: a cliché is the prose equivalent of a poster that you loved when you bought it but that has been hanging on your wall for so long that you don't even notice it anymore.

Among the countless clichés in the English language are phrases like "torrential downpour" (why must it always be *torrential*?), a "striking resemblance" (why not *surprising, astonishing, notable,* or any one of a dozen other appropriate adjectives?), "the crack of dawn," "in this day and age," "when all is said and done," "to vanish into thin air," and "a babbling brook." Many clichés are proverbs, like "Too many cooks spoil the broth" and "Time heals all wounds." And some are metaphors and similes: "good as gold," "happy as a lark," "cool as a cucumber," "smart as a whip," "to sell like hot cakes," and so on. Clichés are so familiar to most of us that we hardly notice how little sense some of them make. Why the *crack* of dawn, for instance? Why vanish into *thin* air? How smart is a whip?

Most personal conversations contain a high proportion of clichés. When two people who have absolutely nothing to say to each other meet on a hot day, you can almost be certain that one of them will say, "Hot enough for you?" and that the other will chime back, "It's not the heat, it's the humidity." An adult meeting a child after a long separation will nearly always say, "My, how you've grown," even if the child hasn't grown an inch.

But what is understandable and excusable in personal conversation is not permissible in written prose. Good writers, therefore, try to avoid clichés in their work. But it's not easy. (For example, in the second sentence of this paragraph, I almost wrote that good writers "try to avoid clichés *like the plague*"—which is, of course, a cliché.) Though they know better, writers often use clichés out of laziness, because the unoriginal is always easier to come up with than the original. The unoriginal is safer, too. And that's a second reason why some beginning writers resort to clichés: because, being too insecure to express their own ideas in their own words, they feel comfortable with clichés that they have heard again and again.

But a writer who relies upon clichés in this manner is making a mistake. For clichés communicate little. Though easy for a reader to digest, they are "empty calories." Writers who use them indicate by doing so that they have failed to think, that they have made no effort to say something original—or, failing that, to say something familiar in an original way. And if you have nothing to offer but stale ideas expressed in stale language, then there is no point in writing in the first place.

Every composition teacher understands how easy a trap clichés are to fall into. (Did you catch the cliché in that sentence?) Name a commonly assigned undergraduate composition topic, and the appropriate clichés come to mind rapidly. Take "my career plans," for example. Students who are asked to write about this topic, but who don't bother to think about it before writing or are too insecure to say what they really want to say, are likely to string together any number of the following clichés: "Life is what you make it." "I'm going to get out there and win." "You've got to play the game." "When the going gets tough, the tough get going." "You've got to be practical." "You can't have everything you want." "You have to go for it." Ask the same students to write about gun control, and the chances are that if they're against it, they'll say that "guns don't kill, people kill." Ask them to write about capital punishment, and they'll use the expression "an eye for an eye." Ask them to write about forced retirement at age sixty-five and they'll say that "age is only a number" and that "experience is the best teacher."

One subject that occasions innumerable clichés is love. Most love letters are replete with clichés. "I love you more than my life." "You're everything to me." "I'm nothing without you." "If something happened to you, I don't know what I'd do." "How did I live before you came along?" These are charming sentiments, but the language in which they are expressed is so stale that only the beloved is likely to feel their charm. They deserve to be conveyed more vividly, more effectively. Indeed, one of the arts of writing is to convey such sentiments as these—even though they may be as old as the hills (cliché!)—in a way that makes the reader feel no one has ever put them into words before. Another way of saying this is that every new generation must find new ways of saying old things, so that the old things will seem fresh and new.

There *is* one way, however, in which clichés can be of use to a writer. Often a clever twist on an old phrase can help one to make a point effectively. Look at the first sentence of Section 34, for instance.

◆

Use fresh, original language.

31

Sorrowful words become the sorrowful, angry words the passionate, jesting words the merry, and solemn words the grave.
—Horace, *Ars Poetica*

◆

Tone

The **tone** of your writing is to your style as your mood is to your personality. To put it differently: style is what runs through all your work—the tendency to use certain types of words, to write certain types of sentences. Tone, on the other hand, is the approach you take to a specific topic, the attitude you assume toward the matter at hand. Though you may convey this attitude explicitly—for example, by saying in so many words that you hate hospitals, love the stories of Eudora Welty, or find soap operas ridiculous—you should also make your attitude implicit in every sentence that you write.

For instance, in the following passage from an essay called "Texts from Housman," the late poet and critic Randall Jarrell adopts a rather serious, authoritative tone:

> The logic poetry has or pretends to have generally resembles induction more than deduction. Of four possible procedures (dealing entirely with particulars, dealing entirely with generalizations, inferring the relatively general from the relatively particular, and deducing the particular from the more general), the third is very much the most common, and the first and second are limits which "pure" and didactic poetry timidly approach. In this essay I am interested in that variety of the third procedure in which the generalizations are implicit. When such generalizations are simple ones, very plainly implied by the particulars of the poem, there will be little tendency to confuse this variety of the third procedure with the first procedure; when they are neither simple nor very plainly implied, the poem will be thought of as "pure" (frequently, "nature") poetry.

Though he uses the word "I," Jarrell's approach in these sentences is essentially impersonal; he wants to sound sensible and judicious, wants to give the impression that he knows what he is talking about and that he is not voicing a personal bias but a set of critical ideas arrived at as a result of cool, professional deliberation.

In contrast to the tone of the preceding lines is Jarrell's famous essay "Some Lines from Whitman." Here Jarrell is more enthusiastic, less reserved, more personal, less scholarly. He is not interested in impressing the reader with his ability to speak dispassionately on critical matters but, instead, is eager to infect the reader with his own excitement over Whitman's poetry—and over his ideas about it:

> Having wonderful dreams, telling wonderful lies, was a temptation Whitman could never resist; but telling the truth was a temptation he could never resist, either. When you buy him you know what you are buying. And only an innocent and solemn and systematic mind will condemn him for his contradictions: Whiteman's catalogues of evils represent realities, and his denials of their reality represent other realities, of feeling and intuition and desire. If he is faithless to logic, to Reality As It Is—whatever that is—he is faithful to the feel of things, to reality as it seems; this is all that a poet has to be faithful to, and philosophers have been known to leave logic and Reality for it.

The sentences here are looser, more conversational; the groups of words connected by the word *and*—"innocent and solemn and systematic," "feeling and intuition and desire"—have a chatty quality to them; and the expression "whatever that is" refreshingly and charmingly betrays the author's lack of omniscience in a way that would have been inappropriate in the first passage.

In "A Note on Poetry," which first appeared as an introduction to a collection of his poems, Jarrell is even more personal, speaking to the reader as to a friend or confidante; far from assuming a loftily authoritative tone, he is self-effacing and determinedly *un*authoritative, presenting himself as a man who is not quite sure *what* the present occasion calls for, a man who is actually "uncomfortable" in his present role. Note how frequently the word *I* appears:

> I may as well say what the reader will soon enough see, that I don't want to write a preface. I am not even sure what sort I am expected to write: one telling what I meant these poems to be or do, I suppose, along with sections about the function of poetry and its state at present. Now the reader may be interested in what the poems are; but why should he care what I meant them to be? And the thought of saying anything about the function of poetry or its present condition, in a couple of pages, makes me uncomfortable.

What make these three passages different from one another—not different in quality, just *different*—are their tones. Jarrell not only has three different subjects in these passages, he has three different *purposes*. In each passage he adopts a tone that he feels will best serve his present purpose. For instance, in the first passage he has a set of ideas to convey about the topic of poetic logic, and thus it serves his purpose to sound as erudite, as level-headed, and as serious as possible. In the second he also has ideas to convey—but these ideas have nothing to do with systematic logic. On the contrary, in this second passage Jarrell is out to defend Whitman's lack of logic on the grounds that illogical or not, Whitman's poetry *feels* right. Because this is his purpose, his tone here is meant to suggest that he is a reader and lover of poetry to whom feeling has priority over logic—a man who is a human being first, a critic second. And in the third passage, he's most human of all. He wants to introduce himself to the readers of his poetry not as a critical theorist but as a person like themselves who happens to write poetry—a man who puts their own everyday lives and concerns into verse. The tone of each passage, then, is the result of a different set of intentions on Jarrell's part.

The lesson in all this is that each time you sit down to write, you should be conscious of your tone. In most expository essays, of course, you should probably be as objective as possible: leave out your opinions and let your readers make up their own minds about your topic. In many narrative and descriptive essays, on the other hand—and in *all* argumentative essays—you should know not only what you are going to say but how you feel about it and how you want your reader to feel about it.

Most important of all, once you have established a tone, stick to it. Many beginning writers unwittingly commit "tone shifts," usually because they have stopped work on a paper at the end of a day, then resumed work on it the following day, while in a completely different frame of mind. One solution to this problem is to write the entire first draft of a paper at one sitting. If this is not possible, then at least reread what you have already written before you continue writing the next day; that way, presumably, you will be able to write the remainder of the paper in the same tone.

◆

*Choose a tone appropriate to
your paper, and stick to it.*

32

*To write simply is as difficult
as to be good.*
—William Somerset Maugham,
The Summing Up

Simplicity

Accomplished actors know that one of the secrets of good acting is to leave out all unnecessary movements, gestures, inflections—to keep it simple, in other words. The same is true of good dancing, good boxing and basketball playing and water polo, good architecture and carpentry, good surgery, and just about anything else you could name. The fewer moves made to sink a basket, the less electrical cable required to wire a house, the smaller the number of procedures necessary to perform a kidney transplant, the better. And the same goes for writing. In writing, as in all these things, simplicity is a virtue.

This does not mean that the thoughts and ideas you convey in your writing should be simple. It means that, however complex those thoughts and ideas may be, the language in which you express them should be as uncomplicated as possible. Indeed, the more complex your material, the more important it is that you make every effort not to complicate matters still further with needlessly difficult prose. Never forget that the purpose of writing is not to confuse or to impress, but to communicate—to let your reader know, as plainly and precisely as possible, what is on your mind.

Many beginning writers tend to lose sight of this fact. Instead of aiming to present strong, clear ideas in strong, clear language, they attempt to fashion a piece of writing containing as many big words and as many long, complex sentences as possible. Often such writing is the result of insecurity. Beginning writers may feel that their own ideas, thoughts, opinions, and experiences are not good enough or interesting enough, or they may be uncomfortable about expressing their opinions on controversial issues. Or they may not have a clear notion of precisely what they do know.

Does this describe the way you felt about the last paper you had to write? Perhaps you had an idea to express, but deep down you didn't think it was all that great an idea; perhaps you had an opinion to offer, but were uncertain why you held this opinion or unable to explain why; or perhaps you had an argument to present, but recognized subconsciously that it was a weak one, based on shaky logic or erroneous assumptions. And perhaps instead of putting whatever you had to offer in clear, simple language and letting it stand naked before the world, you hid it under a blanket of important-sounding words and elaborate syntactic constructions, hoping that this would keep the weakness of your idea, opinion, or argument from being exposed.

So it goes with many a beginning writer. She says "sanitary engineer" when she means "garbage collector," says "municipality" when she means "city," says "abode" or "domicile" or "residence" when she means "house" or "apartment" (either of which, by the way, would be more specific, and therefore better, than "abode," "domicile," or "residence"). When she wants to say that she disapproves of raising the drinking age to twenty-one, she writes something like this:

> One might reasonably suggest that the widespread advocacy in contemporary American society of the nationwide elevation to twenty-one of the age at which one is legally permitted to purchase and imbibe alcoholic beverages is not sound, as far as judicious considerations are concerned.

There is no reason to write like this. This is not to say there's something wrong with the words in the sentence; they're all good words. It's just that *these* words, in *this* combination, are not necessary to express *this* idea. The forty-three-word sentence is simply a long, nervous, boring way of saying the following:

> Raising the drinking age to twenty-one would be wrong.

And this is, in fact, the way the idea should be phrased.

To write a long sentence where a short one would do just as well is to engage in **wordiness**. Not all wordy sentences are as long and grotesque as the preceding example; all it takes to be wordy is to use *at the present time* instead of *now*, *in the event that* in place of *if*, *until such time as* rather than *until*. Wordy writers describe something as *red in color* or *large in size* when all they need to say is *red* or *large*; they use unnecessary expressions like *has the ability to* or *has a tendency to* and tags like *as far as I am concerned* and *in my opinion*, which can usually be eliminated altogether; and they fill their sentences with abstract nouns (like *area, aspect, process, situation, factor*), lifeless verbs (*occur, exist, happen*), and empty adverbs (*very, extremely, basically, essentially*), which can usually be removed. Take the following sentences, for instance:

> My situation, as it exists at the present time, is that I am basically studying in the field of chemistry.

> The moviemaking process is an extremely fascinating area of inquiry, as far as I am concerned.

> What is happening, essentially, is that the bus drivers are on strike.

These three sentences could be simplified:

> I am now studying chemistry.
>
> Moviemaking fascinates me.
>
> The bus drivers are on strike.

Length alone does not make a sentence wordy; the test is whether all the words are necessary. We would not, for example, want to cut a word of the following:

> Four score and seven years ago, our fathers brought forth on this continent a new nation, conceived in liberty and dedicated to the proposition that all men are created equal.

Sentences that contain the words *there is* or *there are* can often be simplified. Consider the following:

> There is a psychiatrist who works in this building who is famous.

The shorter version of this sentence is much stronger:

> A famous psychiatrist works in this building.

Similarly, the words *that* and *which* are often signs that a sentence is longer than it has to be. Take the following sentence:

Simplicity 211

> This is a movie that I like very much.

This sentence can be changed to:

> I like this movie very much.

When you find yourself trying to swathe an idea or opinion in too many words, stop and ask yourself: Why am I doing this? Why am I trying to hide from this idea or opinion? Why am I trying to hide it from my reader? Usually the answer will be that you haven't really thought enough about your subject. Remind yourself that expressing relatively simple ideas and opinions in relatively complicated language is no way of dealing with the fact that those ideas and opinions may not be sound. When you do this, you're not solving anything: you're just adding another problem—wordiness—to the problem you already have.

So keep it simple. And if your pruning of excess wordage exposes logical flaws, repair those flaws; if it results in prose that sounds like something out of a third-grade reader, combine your sentences to create compound and complex sentences. If it results in a paper that is too brief, the answer is not to add more words but to explore your topic in greater depth.

◆

Avoid wordiness.

33

The sound must seem an echo to the sense.
—Alexander Pope, *Essay on Criticism*

◆

Euphony

Like many words in the English language, *euphony* derives from the ancient Greek. *Eu* is Greek for "good" (thus the name of the rock group The Eurhythmics means "good rhythm") and *phonos* is Greek for "sound" or "voice" (as in "microphone," "telephone," and "phonograph"). So we have *euphony*—"good sound" or "good voice"—which refers to a combination of words that sounds pleasant rather than brash, ugly, discomfiting, or even cacophonous.

Euphony is an important attribute of good prose. This doesn't mean that the sentences you write must sound "pretty"; indeed, if you set out to write "pretty" sentences, you will probably end up with something that merely sounds peculiar and affected. All it means is that you should take care not to write sentences that sound so strange that the reader will pay more attention to the words, to the patterns of vowels and consonants, than to the ideas that they are designed to convey.

One type of error to watch for is unintentional *alliteration* or *assonance*. Alliteration is the repetition of consonant sounds. It can be effective in poetry (as in Shakespeare's line, "Full fathom five thy father lies") and it can even (on rare occasions) be used to good effect in prose; but all too often, when it appears in prose, it is merely distracting and unpleasant. For example, consider the following sentence, with its repeated *w* sound:

> Woodrow Wilson's one wish was to save the world from the woes of war.

This sentence contains eight words with an initial *w* sound (that includes the word *one*). Most of these words can easily be eliminated by using synonyms. Here are two ways to rewrite the sentence:

> Woodrow Wilson's great desire was to save the world from war.
>
> Woodrow Wilson's profoundest hope was to help eliminate the conditions that led to war.

Assonance, which is also used widely in poetry, is the repetition of vowel sounds. Like alliteration, it is all too frequently an enemy of good prose rather than a friend, and it can creep into a sentence quite silently when a writer is not alert:

> Though the plays of Noel Coward aren't endowed with great dramatic power, they can provide a pleasant way to spend a couple of hours.

Though the assonance here is perhaps not as offensive as the alliteration in the Woodrow Wilson sentence, the repeated *ow* sound in "Coward," "endowed," "power," and "hours" should be eliminated. This is easily done:

> Though the plays of Noel Coward have little dramatic force, they offer a pleasant way to spend an evening.

Another kind of error to guard against is the unintentional use of rhyming words, particularly adjacent to one another:

> The popularity of President Ford soared after the Mayagüez incident.

"Ford" rhymes with "soared." The easiest way to fix this sentence is to find a synonymous word or expression to take the place of "soared":

> The popularity of President Ford rose dramatically after the Mayagüez incident.

One of the most common types of unintentional rhymes in prose involves the repetition of certain familiar word endings, such as the tags *-ing* and *-tion:*

> The system of education in our nation is in a very perilous situation.

Notice the repeated *-tion* ending. Again, a couple of slight changes will do the trick:

> The American educational system is on the verge of catastrophe.

Thanks to these changes, the unpleasant echo of the *-tion* ending has been avoided. And the sentence—no longer encumbered by unintentional patterns of sound that may well distract the reader from its meaning—is stronger as a result.

◆

Rid your prose of distracting and unintentional echoes and rhymes.

34

*Be choak'd with such another
Emphasis.*
—William Shakespeare, *Antony
and Cleopatra*

◆

Emphasis

Some parts of every paragraph—and, by the same token, some parts of every sentence—are more important than others. In almost every sentence, there are one or two key words, words that are most instrumental in carrying the sentence's meaning. At the same time, there are established ways of making it clear to your readers which words are the important ones—ways, that is, of directing emphasis. Consider the following sentence, for example:

> Rob worked after school every day for three years in order to save enough money to buy the car of his dreams, but the money disappeared the day before he was going to buy the car.

This sentence communicates an interesting anecdote. But because the writer has failed to direct emphasis properly, the anecdote isn't as interesting as it might be.

What can be done to improve it? Let's look at the anecdote more closely and ask ourselves: What makes this piece of information interesting? What is it, in other words, that we should emphasize?

What makes this anecdote interesting, clearly, is the abrupt reversal of Rob's fortunes. One minute he had all that hard-earned money; the next minute he had nothing. He underwent, in short, a dramatic change in circumstances—and the problem with the sentence, as written, is that it simply isn't structured dramatically enough to do this reversal justice. What the sentence should undergo, plainly, is an abrupt shift to emphasize the abrupt shift in Rob's circumstances.

The writer of the sentence has failed to recognize this. Instead, he has merely separated the sentence's two parts with a comma. The comma is correct, grammatically, but it doesn't serve the sentence's stylistic needs; one way to serve these needs—to provide the appropriate emphasis—is to change the comma to a semicolon:

> Rob worked after school every day for three years in order to save enough money to buy the car of his dreams; but the money disappeared the day before he was going to buy the car.

Here the semicolon is an improvement over the comma, because the semicolon emphasizes the sentence's abrupt shift more strongly than the comma does. A period provides even stronger emphasis:

> Rob worked after school every day for three years in order to save enough money to buy the car of his dreams. But the money disappeared the day before he was going to buy the car.

One way to direct emphasis to the relationship between two clauses, then, is to separate them with a semicolon or period rather than a comma.

But our sentence about the fortunes of Rob—which is now two sentences—can be improved still further. The thing to do is to look for important words in the two sentences that are not receiving as much emphasis as they should. Unquestionably, the most important words in the second sentence are "the money disappeared." These words form the main clause of the sentence; it is a "loose" sentence, the type of complex sentence in which the main clause *precedes* the subordinate clause or clauses. A good way to add emphasis to the main clause in such a case is to transform the sentence into a "periodic" sentence, in which the main clause *follows* the subordinate clause or clauses:

> Rob worked after school every day for three years in order to save enough money to buy the car of his dreams. But, the day before he was going to buy the car, the money disappeared.

Clearly, this is an improvement. Placing words at the end of a sentence, in fact, always gives them added emphasis.

Placing words at the beginning of a sentence is almost, though not quite, as effective. We might rearrange the elements in the first of the two quoted sentences, for instance, in order to emphasize the amount of time Rob spent working:

> For three years, Rob worked after school every day in order to save enough money to buy the car of his dreams. But, the day before he was going to buy the car, the money disappeared.

By leading off with the words "For three years," we stress Rob's perseverance.

We might even make the first of these two sentences periodic:

> In order to save enough money to buy the car of his dreams, Rob worked after school every day for three years. But, the day before

> he was going to buy the car, the money disappeared.

The first sentence is more emphatic this way. Since it's periodic, the main clause ("Rob worked after school . . . ") is emphasized, with the words "for three years" getting special emphasis by virtue of their placement at the end of the sentence.

Yet we have done something here that may not be wise: we've written two periodic sentences in a row. Why is this perhaps unwise? Because overusing periodic sentences dissipates their effectiveness. Use them too frequently and you don't create emphasis, you just create monotony. So perhaps we are better off keeping the first of the two sentences loose, the second periodic.

But this is not to say that the emphasis in these two sentences cannot be further improved. Consider the following:

> Rob worked after school every day for three years in order to save enough money to buy the car of his dreams. But the day before he was going to buy the car, tragedy struck—the money disappeared.

Here we've employed a dash to set off the words "the money disappeared" (and, in order to do so, we've added two words). The dash further emphasizes the disappearance of the money. But, as with periodic sentences, overuse of the dash can hinder its effectiveness:

> Rob worked after school every day for three years—three years!—in order to save enough money to buy the car of his dreams. But the day before he was going to buy the car, tragedy struck—the money disappeared.

Under the circumstances, use of the dash to set off the words "three years!" might be acceptable. But in this instance its main effect is to draw attention away from the disappearance of the money, and thus ruin the impact of the final dash. So we are perhaps best off with just the one dash at the end.

Or are we? Do we even want to keep that dash? For an even more effective way of setting off the words "the money disappeared" is to make them a separate, short sentence. For a sudden shift from long or medium-length sentences to a single short sentence is an excellent way of directing emphasis:

> Rob worked after school every day for three years in order to save enough money to buy the car of his dreams. But the day before he was going to buy the car, tragedy struck. The money disappeared.

Note how a longer sentence at the end would not be nearly as emphatic:

> Rob worked after school every day for three years in order to save enough money to buy the car of his dreams. But the day before he was going to buy the car, tragedy struck. He went to his bureau, opened the top drawer,

and discovered that the money had disappeared.

Nor does an exclamation point help. Though it seems an easy way of adding emphasis to a sentence, the exclamation point is almost always uncomfortably reminiscent of the dialogue in Batman comic books:

> Rob worked after school every day for three years in order to save enough money to buy the car of his dreams. But the day before he was going to buy the car, tragedy struck. The money disappeared!

What about italics? They can be effective for emphasis, but must be used with care. Resort to them only when there is no other grammatically and stylistically acceptable way to provide heightened emphases. (Note the places where I've used italics in this section. Can you see why I've used them?)

We've seen that placing words at the end of a sentence directs emphasis toward them. Likewise, for a list of items, proper emphasis is usually served by putting the most important item last:

> Rob wracked his brain, wondering if he had mislaid the money in his house, or if his dog Rusty had buried it in the yard, or if it had been stolen.

Because the possibility of theft is the most chilling of the three, it comes last here. But the emphasis in

Emphasis 223

this sentence can be improved by substituting questions for statements:

> Rob wracked his brain. Had he mislaid the money in the house? Had his dog Rusty buried it in the yard? Or had it been stolen?

The last sentence in the preceding quotation can be improved still further. It's in the "passive voice," meaning that the subject of the sentence—here, the word *it*, referring to Rob's money—is not the performer of the action (that is, stealing) but is the recipient of it. Changing the passive voice to the more common "active voice"—in which the subject performs the action—makes a sentence more emphatic:

> Rob wracked his brain. Had he mislaid the money in the house? Had his dog Rusty buried it in the yard? Or had somebody stolen it?

Here *somebody* is the subject, *had . . . stolen* is the verb; the concluding sentence is thus in the active voice, and is more emphatic.

Another way to direct emphasis is by using a key word more than once.

> Rob acted immediately. He searched the house, searched the garage, searched the trunk of his father's car.

Remember, though, not to apply these methods indiscriminately—or to overuse any of them. Know which words, phrases, and themes you want to emphasize. And understand, too, that emphasis is equally important on the large scale. For example, in a paper a major subtopic should receive more space than a minor subtopic; an anecdote used to illustrate a less-than-crucial point should not take many sentences to relate. To ensure that the overall emphasis of a paper is not misdirected, often it may be necessary to trim some paragraphs and to expand others by exploring new avenues of development. Learn to ask yourself not only "What things do I want to say in this paper?" but "How important is the saying of *this* thing compared to the saying of *that* thing?" Don't go on and on about an unimportant subtopic just because you find it fascinating; likewise, don't slight more important subtopics just because they bore or confuse you, or because you feel uncomfortable dealing with them.

In short, always make sure that your reader knows which words, sentences, themes, and observations in your paper are most important, which are less important, and which are least important. The firmer your grasp of these matters, the more effective your writing will be.

◆

*Direct emphasis by manipulating
word order and punctuation.*

35

Why, this is without parallel, this.
—Ben Jonson, *Every Man Out of His Humour*

◆

Parallelism

Wherever one of the five **coordinating conjunctions**—*and, or, nor, but,* or *yet*—appears in a sentence (except at the very beginning), the rules of grammar require that the sentence elements connected by the conjunction be "parallel."

To describe two or more words in a sentence as parallel is to say that they are the same part of speech and that they bear an identical grammatical relationship to the rest of the sentence. In the sentence "Cory likes dogs and cats," for example, the nouns *dogs* and *cats* are parallel because both are objects of the verb *like*—they are both things that Cory likes. Similarly, in the sentence "Cory breeds and trains dogs," the verbs *breeds* and *trains* are parallel because they both describe what Cory does with dogs; and in "Cory and Monique train dogs," the proper nouns *Cory* and *Monique* are parallel.

Not only words, but clauses and phrases as well, can be parallel. In the sentence "Cory likes dogs but Monique likes cats," the clause *Cory likes dogs* is parallel to the clause *Monique likes cats*. All that is necessary for two phrases to be parallel is that they be the same sort of phrase and that they be connected by a coordinating conjunction. What this means, really, is that for two phrases to be parallel they must begin with the same part of speech. Take this sentence, for example:

Cory hates dogs that bite and cats with fleas.

This sentence names two things that Cory hates. One is *dogs that bite*. The other is *cats with fleas*. *Dogs that bite* consists of a noun, a pronoun, and a verb; *cats with fleas* consists of a noun, a preposition, and another noun. But all that matters is that both elements begin with nouns, and are therefore properly parallel.

"Faulty parallelism" is what results when a writer mistakenly uses a coordinating conjunction to connect two elements that are not truly parallel. Here's an example:

> Cory likes to hunt with dogs and playing with cats.

The problem here is that the two elements connected by the word *and*—*to hunt with dogs* and *playing with cats*—are not parallel. *To hunt* is an infinitive; *playing* is a gerund (the *-ing* form of the verb). To eliminate this inconsistency, we may use two gerunds:

> Cory likes hunting with dogs and playing with cats.

Or we may use two infinitives:

> Cory likes to hunt with dogs and play with cats.

Note that I've said *play* instead of *to play*. The logic here is that the *to* following *likes* applies to both *hunt* and *play*. For purposes of clarity, however, we may add the extra *to:*

> Cory likes to hunt with dogs and to play with cats.

Another common error results when a writer forgets that different adjectives often call for different prepositions. Consider the following sentence, for example:

> Monique has always been interested and sensitive to animals.

Since *interested* must be followed by the preposition *in*, not *to*, the sentence should read as follows:

> Monique has always been interested in and sensitive to animals.

In many sentences, parallel structures are indicated by the use of certain pairs of words called **correlative conjunctions.** These include *both/and, either/or, neither/nor,* and *not only/but also.* Here are some examples:

> *Both* Cory *and* Monique have goldfish at home.
> *Neither* Cory *nor* Monique has a canary.
> *Not only* does Cory have goldfish *but* he *also* has an eel.

Some other sets of words that often link parallel elements are *if/then, the/the, the more/the more, that/and that, who/and who,* and *which/and which.* A familiar type of faulty parallelism occurs when writers mistakenly begin a clause with the words *and that, and who* or *and which,* even though no preceding clause begins with *that, who,* or *which:*

> What Monique likes most about cats is their independence and that they are clean.

Here is one way of resolving this inconsistency:

> What Monique likes most about cats is their
> independence and cleanliness.

Now *independence* and *cleanliness,* both nouns, are parallel. Here's another solution:

> What Monique likes most about cats is that
> they are clean and independent.

Now *clean* and *independent,* both adjectives, are parallel. And here's yet another solution:

> What Monique likes most about cats is that
> they are clean and that they can take care
> of themselves.

Now *that they are clean* and *that they can take care of themselves,* both clauses beginning with the word *that,* are parallel. And consider this sentence:

> When I met Monique, I realized that she was
> a woman of wit, sensitivity, and who was
> always cheerful.

The *that* here is perfectly acceptable; the problem is with the words *and who.* These words should not be here because the sentence contains no preceding clause beginning with the word *who.* The sentence may be corrected as follows:

> When I met Monique, I realized that she was
> a woman of wit, sensitivity, and constant
> cheerfulness.

Now we have three nouns, all parallel to each other, and no unnecessary *and who.* Note that the adjective *constant*, which modifies *cheerfulness*, does not disrupt the parallelism. There would be trouble, however, if the three nouns were in another sequence:

> When I met Monique, I realized that she was a woman of constant cheerfulness, wit, and sensitivity.

Here it is not clear whether *constant* is meant to modify all three nouns that follow it or to modify *cheerfulness* alone.

Here's another way to correct the sentence:

> When I met Monique, I realized that she was a woman who was witty, sensitive, and cheerful.

Here the three adjectives are parallel. And here's one last possibility:

> When I met Monique, I realized that she was a woman of wit and sensitivity, and that she was always cheerful.

Here the two clauses, both beginning with *that*, are parallel.

As the preceding sentence about Monique demonstrates, one set of parallel sentence elements can exist within another. Consider the following:

> When Monique goes on vacation, she always takes along her five goldfish, her six turtles, and her two cats, Pyramus and Thisbe.

There are two sets of parallel elements here. One set consists of three items, all beginning with the word *her: her five goldfish, her six turtles,* and *her two cats, Pyramus and Thisbe.* The word *and* preceding *her two cats* indicates that this is the last item in this particular series. The other set consists of two items: *Pyramus and Thisbe.* Again, the word *and* appears here as a connective. Clearly, both *and*s in this sentence are necessary: each links the elements in one of the sentence's two parallel structures.

Unfortunately, many types of faulty parallelism are occasioned by such sentences as the one quoted. Many a writer, when confronted with the task of framing a sentence that contains two sets of parallel elements, inadvertently omits or misplaces a coordinating conjunction. Consider the following sentence, for example:

> When I met Monique, I realized that she was witty, sensitive, and had a cheerful disposition.

Witty and *sensitive* are adjectives, and therefore are properly parallel; but *had a cheerful disposition* is not an adjective, and should not be coordinated with these words. The solution is to add another *and* to the sentence, between *with* and *sensitive* (and to omit the commas):

> When I met Monique, I realized that she was witty and sensitive and had a cheerful disposition.

This does the trick. Now *witty* and *sensitive* are parallel, linked by the first *and* in the sentence; and *was witty and sensitive* and *had a cheerful disposition*—two verbs and their objects—are also parallel, linked by the second *and*. The sentence is fixed.

Or is it? Do you notice the ambiguity, the possibility of confusion? A reader might be confused as to whether the words *had a cheerful disposition* are parallel to *was witty and sensitive* or to *realized that she was witty and sensitive*. Who, in other words, had a cheerful disposition—Monique or the sentence's speaker?

In order to make the meaning of this sentence clearer, we may rewrite it as follows:

> When I met Monique, I realized that she was witty and sensitive and that she had a cheerful disposition.

Now both of the larger parallel elements begin with the words *that she*. The meaning is clear.

In many cases, the addition of such words and phrases can serve to avoid this sort of confusion. In other instances, even though there is no such possibility of ambiguity, such additions can help emphasize the parallelism. Consider this sentence:

> Monique has taught me to face the world with a smile, be considerate of animals, and do unto others as I would have them do unto me.

Here the three verb infinitives—*face, be, do*—are parallel. The way the sentence is framed, the word *to* that precedes *face* is meant to apply to all three infinitives. But though the sentence, as it appears above, is grammatically acceptable, it is clearer and more elegant if the additional *to*s are included:

> Monique has taught me to face the world with a smile, to be considerate of animals, and to do unto others as I would have them do unto me.

Parallelism is not only a grammatical requirement, then, but also a valuable stylistic device. It helps to clarify the relationships between ideas or objects and it allows writers to express their thoughts with precision and force.

◆

Ensure that all sentence elements connected by a conjunction are parallel.

36

"Use not vain repetitions."
—The Gospel According to St. Matthew, 6:7

◆

Repetition and Synonyms

Repetition, in writing, is unavoidable. For every topic that you may choose to write about, there will be certain words that you find yourself using again and again. If you are writing about child rearing, for instance, the words *parent* and *child* will doubtless keep cropping up; if your subject is architecture, the word *building* may recur frequently.

There's nothing wrong with this: repetition is no crime. It can, on the contrary, be an effective stylistic tool. I've described (in Section 7) how the deliberate repetition of key words often makes an essay more coherent. But that is not its only advantage; it can also serve to emphasize and dramatize important points. Many memorable pieces of writing, in fact, are memorable precisely because of the skillful use the author makes of repetition. Consider this passage from John F. Kennedy's Inaugural Address, for instance:

> Let both sides explore what problems unite us instead of belaboring those problems which divide us.
>
> Let both sides, for the first time, formulate serious and precise proposals for the inspection and control of arms, and bring the absolute power to destroy other nations under the absolute control of all nations.
>
> Let both sides seek to invoke the wonders of science instead of its terrors. Together let us explore the stars, conquer the deserts, eradicate disease, tap the ocean depths and encourage the arts and commerce.
>
> Let both sides unite to heed in all corners of the earth the command of Isaiah to "undo the heavy burdens . . . [and] let the oppressed go free."

And consider, likewise, this passage from Martin Luther King's address delivered during the 1963 March on Washington:

> I say to you today, my friends, even though we face the difficulties of today and tomorrow, I still have a dream. It is a dream deeply rooted in the American dream. I have a dream that one day this Nation will rise up and live out the true meaning of its creeds—"we hold these truths to be self-evident that all men are created equal."
>
> I have a dream that one day on the red hills of Georgia the sons of slaves and the sons of former slaveowners will be able to sit down together at the table of brotherhood. I have a dream that one day even the state of Mississippi, sweltering with the heat of injustice, sweltering with the heat of oppression, will be transformed into an oasis of freedom and justice.
>
> I have a dream that my four little children will one day live in a Nation where they will not be judged by the color of their skins, but by the content of their character.

Both of these passages are examples of highly charged political rhetoric, in which stylized and insistent repetition is in keeping with their solemn, dramatic tone. To repeat quite so dramatically and insistently, however, in a freshman composition on "My Favorite Sport," say, or "The Rise and Fall of Rock and Roll" would be inappropriate. Yet repetition of a somewhat more subdued sort can still be effective:

> More than any other sport, I like swimming. To swim is to exercise one's en-

tire body, to put every muscle to work, to build up one's strength in a completely natural way. To swim is to feel free and alone, in touch with nature, independent of the land, in contact with nothing except air and water. To swim is to feel oneself returning, in some sense, to one's watery origins—the womb? the sea out of which our amphibian ancestors crawled? Other sports require one to fight, to lash out, to compete with one's fellow human beings; to swim is not to enter into competition but to enter, rather, into a calm yet exhilarating sense of unity with oneself and with nature.

Intentional and purposeful repetition, then, can be quite effective, attracting emphasis to the main points that the writer wants to make. But the careless and unnecessary reiteration of words and phrases can be exceedingly monotonous and can distract the reader from the writer's information and ideas. Such inadvertent repetition, which is frequently accompanied by careless prose, makes a writer look foolish and inattentive.

If you find yourself using a word too many times, then, omit it where possible. If the word still seems too prevalent, find a suitable synonym or synonymous expression. There is no excuse for such tediously repetitious writing as the following:

> In 1920 F. Scott Fitzgerald published his first novel, *This Side of Paradise*. Then in 1922 he published his second novel, *The Beautiful and Damned*. In 1925 he published his

> third novel, *The Great Gatsby*. And in 1934 he published his fourth novel, *Tender Is the Night*.

Not only does the word *published* appear four times in this passage, but all four sentences are structured almost identically. In the preceding passage on swimming, the deliberate repetition of the word *swim* and of sentence structure was stylistically effective; here, however, the lazy, careless repetition of the word *published* and of sentence structure has quite the opposite impact. The repetition bores and irritates the reader. In this case, three of the four appearances of the word *published* can be eliminated:

> In 1920 F. Scott Fitzgerald published his first novel, *This Side of Paradise*. He followed it in 1922 with *The Beautiful and Damned*, in 1925 with *The Great Gatsby*, and in 1934 with *Tender Is the Night*.

Here it is easy enough to reduce the number of appearances of the word *published*. The same is not true of the following passage:

> In 1922 several important works of literature were published. *Ulysses*, by James Joyce, was published by Sylvia Beach's Shakespeare & Co.; *Jacob's Room*, by Virginia Woolf, was published by the Hogarth Press; and *The Waste Land*, by T. S. Eliot, was published in the first issue of his journal, *The Criterion*.

In this case, synonyms are useful:

> In 1922 several important works of literature appeared. Sylvia Beach's Shakespeare & Co. published James Joyce's novel *Ulysses*; the Hogarth Press brought out Virginia Woolf's *Jacob's Room*; and the first issue of T. S. Eliot's journal *The Criterion* contained his poem *The Waste Land*.

Many of the words most frequently used in writing have **synonyms** that, at times, can be used as substitutes to avoid a jarring, distracting echo. For instance, take the word *clearly* in the following passage:

> Katharine Hepburn has been nominated for nine Academy Awards in acting, and has won four—more than any other actor or actress. Clearly, she is one of the major performers of our time.

Let's say you've already used the word *clearly* in this paragraph, and don't want to use it again; in this instance it could be replaced by *patently, manifestly,* or *obviously*. Similarly, *for example* can be replaced by *for instance, in fact* by *indeed*. One particularly good thing about hunting for synonyms to replace overused words is that we often find a better, more precise word for the purpose. Looking for a synonym to replace that overused word *interesting*, for example, we may be forced to decide *in what way* the matter under discussion is interesting, and may consequently find a more specific (or at least more interesting) word—anything from *provocative* to *diverting* to *tantalizing* to *engrossing* to *absorbing* to *enthralling* to *arresting*. . . . It's a rich language.

Because it is so rich, there's no excuse for writing something like this:

> Katharine Hepburn, a very sharp-witted actress with a reputation for being very tough, has always played characters who are very independent.

The use of the word *very* three times in this sentence makes it very, very, very flat. What if we press a few synonyms into service?

> Katharine Hepburn, a remarkably sharp-witted actress with a reputation for being uncommonly tough, has always played characters who are extremely independent.

This is better. But it's not perfect: the sentence is a bit adverb-heavy, weighed down by that repeated adverb-adjective formula. For variety's sake, it might be wise to trade in one of the adverbs for an adverbial phrase and to eliminate the one that does the least work:

> Katharine Hepburn, a sharp-witted actress with a reputation for being uncommonly tough, has always played characters who are independent in the extreme.

Synonyms, then, can be useful. Always make certain, however, that the synonym you choose for a given word is *really* a synonym—and that it is appropriate for the particular use that you wish to make of it. Make certain, too, that you are always using as precise a word as possible to express your meaning; if you must repeat a word in order to retain this precision, then do so.

And be aware that a thesaurus can be an enemy as well as a friend. It can be useful when you know that there is a word with the exact meaning for your purpose, but your memory refuses to yield it up. Yet many student writers misuse the thesaurus. They assume that all the words under a given heading have the same meaning, and therefore may be used interchangeably. This is an error, for there are few words in the English language that mean precisely the same thing. A writer who carelessly uses the synonyms of *very*, for example, might come up with something like this:

> Katharine Hepburn, an enormously sharp-witted actress with a reputation for being incredibly tough, has always played astonishingly independent characters.

A discerning reader will recognize this sentence as the work of a writer who has resorted to the thesaurus, and done so without much care. The adverbs the writer has chosen here are inappropriate modifiers for these particular adjectives. Is Hepburn, after all, actually *incredibly* tough? Look up the word *incredible* in the dictionary; it means "surpassing belief: too extraordinary and improbable to admit of belief." Certainly Hepburn isn't *that* tough. And are her characters so independent as to *astonish* anyone? Perhaps one or two of them are—but *all* of them?

Let's say you're writing a paper about architecture. You find yourself using the word *building* too often and want to do something about it. So you open your thesaurus and find the following synonyms for *building: structure, edifice, construction, construct, erection, establishment, architecture, fabric.* Now, a couple of these words, in a pinch, could possibly be used as a synonym for *building. Edifice* or *structure* would be appropriate, for instance, if you were focusing upon the process of construction. But most (if not all) of the others—if incorporated into a sentence where all that is called for is the word *building*—might well cause readers confusion, even amusement, and would, at the very least, distract them from whatever you have to say about architecture.

There are times, however, when it is not merely advisable but essential to seek out a synonym. One such occasion is when you find yourself using the same word in two different senses within a single brief passage. For instance:

> In my history class, I learned about class conflict.

The word *class* means two different things in this sentence. No one should be confused by this, but a reader might well be jarred momentarily by the shift from one type of class to another. Thus, it's necessary to replace the repeated word, in at least one instance, with a synonym:

> In my history course, I learned about class conflict.

◆

Remember the ways in which repetition and synonyms can be used to make your prose more effective.

37

*Variety is the mother of
Enjoyment.*
—Benjamin Disraeli, *Vivian Gray*

◆

Variety

Variety may be the spice of life, but it is the meat and potatoes of writing. Certain aspects of any piece of writing should be consistent: *style, tone, level of diction.* But—unless they want their readers to die of boredom—writers should be equally careful *not* to be consistent in the length and type of the sentences that they write. Many student writers make the mistake of filling their compositions with simple sentences, as demonstrated by the following paragraph:

> The Irish language seems to be suffering the fate of Morocco's Atlas lions. These lions are now extinct in the wild. But they propagate in captivity. There still exist in Ireland a significant minority. These people frequently speak Irish with family and friends, at home and on the street. They are also fluent in English. As a proportion of the total population, their number appears to be holding steady. They form about ten percent of the population. However, Ireland's Irish-speakers are increasingly not found in the rural Gaeltacht. That is where the language is indigenous. Rather, they are found in Ireland's cities. The language has been transplanted and bred in the cities. The Irish speakers no longer come from the lower strata of Irish society, from the ranks of the farmers and fishermen. These people gave Irish its reputation as a "backward" language. Instead the Irish speakers come more and more from the ranks of the middle class. In particular, they come from the ranks of the white-collar professionals, intellectuals, and bureaucrats of Dublin. This shift is indicated by census data. It is also indicated by a recent survey published in 1984 by the Institiuid Teangeolaiothta Eireann (ITE).

> This semigovernmental agency is responsible for linguistic research.

This passage consists entirely of simple sentences. None of them is badly written, but when strung end-to-end, they form a paragraph that is badly written. The problem created by this succession of simple sentences is twofold: first, it is monotonous; second, it fails to direct emphasis sharply enough, fails to indicate to the reader which of the many points covered in the paragraph are most important. Consider, for instance, the first three sentences of the passage:

> The Irish language seems to be suffering the fate of Morocco's Atlas lions. These lions are now extinct in the wild. But they propagate in captivity.

This brief excerpt from the passage conveys a witty, vivid, and utterly appropriate analogy. But by writing it as three sentences, we may well be confusing the reader; for, though the topic at hand is the Irish language, the fact that the second and third sentences are devoted entirely to the Atlas lions would seem to indicate otherwise. In other words, by giving the lions two sentences of their own we give them more emphasis than they deserve, and probably mislead the reader as to their relative importance in the paragraph. How to solve this problem? Combine the three sentences into one, being careful to subordinate the second and third to the first:

> The Irish language seems to be suffering the fate of Morocco's Atlas lions, which are now extinct in the wild even as they propagate in captivity.

On to the next group of sentences:

> There still exist in Ireland a significant minority. These people frequently speak Irish with family and friends, at home and on the street. They are also fluent in English.

These three sentences can easily be combined into one:

> There still exist in Ireland a significant minority who frequently speak Irish with family and friends, at home and on the street, and who are also fluent in English.

This is an improvement, but it gives too much emphasis to the Irish speakers' fluency in English. The main point that the sentence should make is not that these people speak English but that they speak Irish. So let's recombine the three sentences, relegating the Irish speakers' fluency in English to a more subsidiary position in the sentence.

> There still exist in Ireland a significant minority who, while fluent in English, frequently speak Irish with family and friends, at home and on the street.

That's better. Now let's consider the next two sentences:

> As a proportion of the total population, their number appears to be holding steady. They form about ten percent of the population.

We could combine these two sentences simply by changing the period into a semicolon:

> As a proportion of the total population, their number appears to be holding steady; they form about ten percent of the population.

But the repetition of the phrase *of the population* is unpleasantly distracting. So why not write it as follows?

> As a proportion of the total population, their number appears to be holding steady (at about ten percent).

On to the next group of sentences:

> However, Ireland's Irish-speakers are increasingly not found in the rural Gaeltacht. That is where the language is indigenous. Rather, they are found in Ireland's cities. The language has been transplanted and bred in the cities. The Irish speakers no longer come from the lower strata of Irish society, from the ranks of the farmers and fishermen. These people gave Irish its reputation as a "backward" language. Instead the Irish speakers come more and more from the ranks of the middle class. In particular, they come from the ranks of the professionals, intellectuals, and bureaucrats of Dublin.

There are eight sentences here, but they are not telling us eight different things. Rather, all eight of them hover around one distinct, central fact: that Irish speakers are increasingly likely to come not from the rural lower classes but from the urban middle classes. There are two shifts in one taking place here: a shift from country to city and a shift from the poor to the middle class. It would seem wise to describe these shifts in two sentences, including the most important information (the descriptions of the shifts) in the main clauses and relegating the other material to the subordinate clauses:

> However, Ireland's Irish-speakers are increasingly to be found not in the rural Gaeltacht, where the language is indigenous, but in Ireland's cities, where it has been transplanted and bred. They are being drawn less from the lower strata of Irish society, from the farmers and fishermen who gave Irish its reputation as a "backward" language, and more from the ranks of the middle class, from the white-collar professionals, intellectuals, and bureaucrats of Dublin in particular.

Note that both of these sentences make use of parallel structure in order to describe the shifts. The first sentence follows a "not *A* but *B*" pattern, the second a "less *C* and more *D*" pattern. Note also that the important but secondary historical information (that Irish is indigenous to the Gaeltacht, and that the farmers and fishermen gave Irish its reputation as a "backward" language) is consistently subordinated to the more important information about the present state of linguistic affairs in Ireland.

These two sentences are now much improved. But since they both describe the same cultural phenomenon—since each depends so intimately upon the other—it is probably a good idea to separate them not with a period but with a semicolon, thus combining them into a single long sentence:

> However, Ireland's Irish-speakers are increasingly to be found not in the rural Gaeltacht, where the language is indigenous, but in Ireland's cities, where it has been transplanted and bred; they are being drawn less from the lower strata of Irish society, from the farmers and fishermen who gave Irish its reputation as a "backward" language, and more from the ranks of the middle class, from the white-collar professionals, intellectuals, and bureaucrats of Dublin in particular.

Finally, we have the last three sentences of the paragraph:

> This shift is indicated by census data. It is also indicated by a recent survey published in 1984 by the Instituid Teangeolaiothta Eireann (ITE). This semigovernmental agency is responsible for linguistic research.

These three sentences can be combined into one:

Such are the indications from census data and a recent survey published in 1984 by the Institiuid Teangeolaiothta Eireann (ITE), the semigovernmental agency responsible for linguistic research.

Our paragraph (which, in its final form, has been taken from an essay called "Language: The Irish Question" by Cullen Murphy) now consists not of seventeen thin, wispy simple sentences but of five substantial, well-focused sentences of various types, each of which makes a clear and significant contribution to the paragraph:

> The Irish language seems to be suffering the fate of Morocco's Atlas lions, which are now extinct in the wild even as they propagate in captivity. There still exist in Ireland a significant minority who, while fluent in English, frequently speak Irish with family and friends, at home and on the street. As a proportion of the total population, their number appears to be holding steady (at about ten percent). However, Ireland's Irish-speakers are increasingly to be found not in the rural Gaeltacht, where the language is indigenous, but in Ireland's cities, where it has been transplanted and bred; they are being drawn less from the lower strata of Irish society, from the farmers and fishermen who gave Irish its reputation as a "backward" language, and more from the ranks of the middle class, from the white-collar professionals, intellectuals, and bu-

> reaucrats of Dublin in particular. Such are the indications from census data and a recent survey published in 1984 by the Institiuid Teangeolaiothta Eireann (ITE), the semigovernmental agency responsible for linguistic research.

This paragraph now has variety: of its five sentences, two are simple, two complex, and one compound-complex.

There are other types of variety that are desirable in sentences. For one thing, several sentences in a row should not have the same subject. (The exception to this rule is when you are repeating a subject deliberately for reasons of emphasis.) Consider the following passage:

> Edward M. Kennedy served in the Army, was educated at Harvard, and received his law degree at the University of Virginia. He entered the Senate in 1962, when his brother John was president and his brother Robert was attorney general. He lost his brothers to assassins in 1963 and 1968, respectively, and in turn became a leading contender for the presidency. But he brought an end to that possibility by driving his car off a Chappaquiddick bridge in June of 1969.

The subject of every sentence in this passage is either *Edward M. Kennedy* or the pronoun (*he*) standing for Edward M. Kennedy. The result is monotony—and the solution is to rewrite the passage, varying the subject from sentence to sentence:

> Edward M. Kennedy served in the Army, was educated at Harvard, and received his law degree at the University of Virginia. The voters of Massachusetts elected him to the Senate in 1962, when his brother John was president and his brother Robert was attorney general. John and Robert were assassinated in 1963 and 1968, respectively, leaving Edward as a leading contender for the presidency. But his chances for the White House faded when his car went off a Chappaquiddick bridge in June of 1969.

Here the nicely varied subjects of the four sentences are *Edward M. Kennedy, voters, John and Robert,* and *chances.*

A final kind of variation is worth mentioning. There are four different types of sentences: declarative, imperative, interrogative (ending with a question mark), and exclamatory (ending with an exclamation point). Though the great majority of sentences are—and should be—declarative, it is effective, where appropriate, to convert the occasional declarative sentence into an interrogative sentence:

> Edward M. Kennedy served in the Army, was educated at Harvard, and received his law degree at the University of Virginia. The voters of Massachusetts elected him to the Senate in 1962, when his brother John was

president and his brother Robert was attorney general. John and Robert were assassinated in 1963 and 1968, respectively; and how could younger brother Teddy *not* have become a leading contender for the presidency thereafter? But his chances for the White House faded when his car went off a Chappaquiddick bridge in June of 1969.

Undoubtedly, the question mark gives the paragraph greater variety. But it also lends emphasis to the third sentence, and should therefore only be used if such emphasis is logical and desirable.

◆

Vary sentence length, type, and subject to avoid monotony.

38

*Reading maketh a full man;
conference a ready man; and
writing an exact man.*
—Francis Bacon, *Of Studies*

◆

Specificity

Whenever possible, your written language should be concrete rather than abstract, specific rather than general. *Abstract* words describe concepts or qualities: freedom, trustworthiness, love, life. *Concrete* words describe people, places, things—objects you can see and touch: shirt, car, professor.

Some abstract terms are more specific than others. *Radicalism*, for example, is not as specific as *an-*

archism, which describes a specific type of radicalism. And some concrete terms are more specific than others: *green paisley shirt* is more specific than *shirt*, *Porsche 911 Carrera* is more specific than *car*, and *Professor Vendler* is more specific than *professor*.

Concrete prose is preferable to abstract prose because it makes it possible for your readers to visualize what you are writing about; and the more fully they can visualize it, the less likely they will become bored or confused. Consider the following sentence, for example:

> The Florida climate caused me considerable discomfort.

This sentence contains at least two abstractions: *climate* and *discomfort*. The next sentence is an improved version:

> The Florida heat made me sweat.

Heat, though somewhat abstract, is more specific than *climate* and therefore preferable. And to say that you sweated evokes a concrete image, and is therefore better than merely saying that you were caused great discomfort. But this sentence can be improved still further:

> The 105-degree heat in Coral Gables caused sweat to pour down my face and soak my shirt.

This is more concrete, more specific—and therefore more vivid and interesting.

Of course, sometimes you can't avoid writing in abstract, general terms:

> Life moved slowly that summer.

But if you can, follow up with concrete, specific details:

> Life moved slowly that summer. We rose from our great musty beds every day at noon, dawdled over our ham, eggs, grits, and coffee till mid-afternoon, and spent the long, humid evenings lounging in those old green rockers on the screened-in front porch, swatting at flies and mosquitoes, chewing tobacco, and telling sad stories of the deaths of kings.

The difference between general and specific description is a matter of *observation*. Writers who have nothing to offer but vague, unevocative prose seem to be suggesting that they are not interested enough in what they are writing about to look at it carefully or to render it in compelling visual terms—and if *they're* not interested, why should their readers be? Writers who bring their subjects to life with precise and accurate details, on the other hand, prove thereby that they have observed those subjects with interest—and cannot help but make their readers interested, as well.

Therefore, write as vividly as you can. Use colorful nouns and verbs. Don't, if you can help it, write that "The ten o'clock train went by" or "The ten o'clock train passed by"; *to go* and *to pass* are notoriously dull verbs. How much more lively the statement becomes when you toss in a more specific verb:

> The ten o'clock train rattled by.
> The ten o'clock train sped by.
> The ten o'clock train charged by.

Each of these sentences evokes a vivid picture—and each picture is somewhat different from the others. The first sentence suggests an old, broken-down, slow-moving, noisy freight train; the second suggests a sleek, fast-moving, relatively quiet passenger train, all gleam and efficiency; the third suggests a fast, loud monster of the night.

A good time to remember to be specific is when you find yourself making a value judgment—when you write, for instance, that a certain book is good, a certain movie bad, your car beautiful, your aunt witty, your physics teacher brilliant. Keep in mind that your reader is liable to be curious as to *why* you found the book good, the movie bad, and so on. So be *specific*—tell *why* you feel the way you do:

> Professor Gupta is a brilliant professor. He is able to grasp the most difficult concepts—general relativity, the Big Bang theory—and to explain them in such a way that they don't seem difficult at all.

Don't be afraid of being specific. Details—as long as they are relevant to your discussion—are a boon to any piece of writing. A problem with many essays by student writers is that they simply don't go into enough detail. Consider the following passage, for example:

> In the late fifties, a mob of Bolivians, enraged at a story in *Time* magazine, rioted at the American embassy in Bolivia. *Time* had quoted an unnamed U.S. embassy official as saying that America had spent a lot of money in Bolivia without effect, adding that the only solution was to dissolve Bolivia and to divide it and its problems up among its neighbors. The Bolivian cabinet met to consider measures to restore order, and Americans were evacuated for their own safety. The Bolivian ambassador to the U.S. expressed his concern over the article to the American Secretary of State. American embassy people in Bolivia denied having made the statement "quoted" by *Time*. The magazine's editor issued a statement regretting the violence but admitting no error on the part of *Time*.

As it stands, this is a well-developed paragraph. But it is not quite as vigorous or vivid as it might be. What it lacks is specificity of detail. One wonders: *When* in the late fifties did this happen? How big was the mob? What did they do at the riot? What were the consequences? How much money, according to *Time*, had the U.S. spent in Bolivia? What exactly did that embassy official supposedly say? Who was the American Secretary of State at the time? And so forth. Compare the following version of the same paragraph:

> In March 1959, some 10,000 Bolivians, enraged at a *Time* story, stoned the American embassy in La Paz, burned copies of *Time* along with the American flag, and rioted until two of their number were killed. *Time* had quoted an unnamed U.S. embassy official as saying that America had spent $129 million in Bolivia without effect, adding jocularly that the only solution was to "abolish Bolivia and let its neighbors divide the country and its problems among themselves." The Bolivian cabinet met to consider measures to restore order, while hundreds of Americans were evacuated to an army camp for their own safety. The Bolivian ambassador in Washington called on Secretary of State Christian Herter to express concern over the article. American embassy people in La Paz denied having made the statement "quoted" by *Time*. [*Time* publisher] Henry Luce issued a statement regretting the violence but admitting no *Time* error.

The added details in this revised version of the paragraph (which, I should add, is adapted from W. A. Swanberg's biography, *Luce and His Empire*) improve it in a couple of ways. For one thing they make it richer and more vivid; the information is more compelling and the riot easier to visualize. For another thing, the added details make the writer appear to be in greater command of his subject. He knows the date of the riot, the number of Bolivians involved, and so on—the sort of thing that increases a reader's respect for a writer.

There is, however, such a thing as going overboard with details. A particular danger is that of including irrelevant details—details, that is, which would tend to distract a reader from the central topic of a paragraph. If, in the featured passage, the details are all effective, it is because they are related to the paragraph's theme. But one can easily imagine a writer overdoing it a bit:

> At ten-thirty on the cloudy morning of March 3, 1959, some 10,000 Bolivians, enraged at a *Time* story entitled "Those Nutty Bolivians," stoned the three-story, red-brick American embassy at 55 Avenida Don Quixote in La Paz, which had been designed by the architect Sam Lewis. These rioters also burned 59 copies of *Time* and an American flag, and rioted until two of their number were killed—Carlos Ordoñes, 29, a tin miner, and Guillermo Andujar, 45, an astronomy professor at the University of La Paz. *Time* had quoted an unnamed U.S. embassy official as saying that America had spent $129 million in Bolivia without effect, adding jocularly that the only solution was to "abolish Bolivia and let its neighbors divide the country and its problems among

themselves." Those neighbors include Peru, Brazil, Paraguay, and Chile. The Bolivian cabinet met in the dark-paneled Cabinet Room at the Presidential Mansion on the Avenida de la Liberacion, and considered measures to restore order. Meanwhile 583 Americans were evacuated to Camp Wanda Hendrix for their own safety. The Bolivian ambassador in Washington, the tall, blue-eyed tin magnate Emilio San Vicente, called on Secretary of State Christian Herter (Yale, '32) at his palatial estate in Maryland to express concern over the article. . . .

Et cetera. I have concocted most of the added information, but the idea should be clear: that the introduction of all this irrelevant detail into the paragraph does not improve it but, on the contrary, robs it of its focus.

◆

> *Prefer the concrete to the abstract, the specific to the general.*

39

Proper words in proper places make the true definition of a style.
—Jonathan Swift, *Letter to a Young Clergyman*

♦

Appropriate Diction

Diction means "use of words." Each time you sit down to write, you make a decision, consciously or unconsciously, as to the sort of words you are going to use. Since the English language has the largest vocabulary of any language in the world, you have a much wider field to choose from than does a student in China or Sweden or Morocco. For instance, consider the number of synonyms we have in English for the word *clothing: clothes, apparel, wear, dress, raiment, garb, garments, clobber, duds, costume, costumery, attire, getup, array, rig, habit, habiliments, guise, gear, vestments, togs, uniform, toggery, threads.* How are you to know which word to use?

In part, the decision is a matter of personal style. Where one writer would use the word *clothing,* another might use the word *apparel,* and neither would be more correct than the other. But the decision should also be based upon other factors. Among these factors are the topic you are writing about, the audience you are writing to, and the level of formality that you want to achieve. For while *clothing, clothes, apparel, attire,* and *garments* are all commonly used words that would not be out of place in any piece of writing, many of the other synonyms are rarely used, at least as synonyms for *clothing.* (*Habit* and *vestments,* for example, are generally employed only to describe items worn by clergy and members of religious orders.) If you were to use these words as synonyms for *clothing,* then, you would have to have a special reason for doing so, a certain effect that you wanted to convey. What makes each of these words valuable is that each has a unique set of **connotations**—a set of ideas and feelings, that is, that the word suggests. If you wanted to poke gentle fun at a person's dandyish way of dressing, for instance, you might use the word *costumery;* if you wanted to affect a lofty (or mock-lofty) tone, you might use *habiliments*; if you wanted to affect an informal, rather humorous manner, you might use *threads* or *duds* or *togs* or *rig*, all of which are colloquial; if you were writing dialogue for a Cockney, you might use *clobber*, which is British slang.

What is meant by colloquial and slang? **Colloquial** words are those which are used by educated, intelligent people in conversation and in personal letters, but which should be avoided in formal writing. The long roster of colloquial words in English includes *dumb* (when used to mean *stupid*), *lousy* (when used to mean *bad*), *guy* (when used to mean *male*), and *jerk* (when used to mean *fool*). The difference between colloquial language and slang is that colloquial words are here to stay—for a few more decades, at least—whereas slang words may be gone by next year. **Slang** is the informal language of the moment. In the sixties, the slang words of the moment included *groovy* and *outasight*; as I write this, the current slang lexicon includes words like *rad* and *crash* (as in "Can I crash at your place?") and expressions like *being into* (as in "I'm into surfing") and *getting off on* (as in "Yeah, I get off on surfing, too").

Though colloquialisms have their place in certain types of writing, avoid using slang in your prose. What looks very up-to-date today may look old-fashioned tomorrow; just as you laugh now at words like *groovy*, so young people a few years hence are likely to laugh at the slang words that your generation uses. A good rule to follow whenever you write anything, then, is to ask yourself: "Twenty years from now, would somebody be able to read this and understand it? Or would the language make it seem dated?"

Besides colloquial and slang words, there's another large chunk of the English vocabulary that goes by the name of **jargon.** Jargon is the language that specialists in a given field use among themselves. Chemists speak of valences and isotopes, literary critics of intertextuality and hermeneutics. Unless you are writing for a specialized audience, however, you should avoid using such language yourself. You may come across a good deal of it while researching a paper, but this doesn't justify your writing that way too; part of your job, in such a case, is to translate the jargon of your sources into plain, simple English that nonspecialists can understand without difficulty. If you *must* use specialized terms, be certain to define them clearly. Remember that when you are writing on any subject, however obscure, for a general audience, the idea is to illuminate. And jargon, when directed at a general audience, tends not to illuminate but to confuse.

What sort of words you use depends, to a large extent, on whether you want to write **formal** or **informal prose.** Formal prose is impersonal—free of first-person singular pronouns (*I, me, my, mine*), free of contractions (*it's, there's,* and so forth), free of colloquialisms. The sentences tend to be rather long and complex. Formal prose is used in scholarly and technical writing, in academic journals and research papers. Informal prose, on the other hand, is relatively freewheeling; colloquialisms, contractions, and first-person pronouns are more common than in formal prose and the sentences tend to be shorter, simpler, looser, and more conversational. Sentence fragments are often used for stylistic purposes. Informal prose is the prose of personal letters, of articles in magazines like *Esquire* and *Cosmopolitan*, and of essays by certain journalists, including William Safire and Russell Baker.

Besides formal and informal prose, there are numerous intermediate levels. In *Time*, for instance, the prose is relatively informal, containing numerous colloquialisms and sentence fragments, but the first-person pronoun is shunned. *The New York Times*, by contrast, is relatively formal, though the sentences are not as complex as in most formal writing. (The style of this book, incidentally, is rather informal.)

Here is an excerpt from a comparatively informal essay by Clancy Sigal, originally published in *New York* magazine, in which he discusses E. L. Doctorow's novel *Loon Lake:*

> For me, *Loon Lake* had its moments. But the style—some of it written in a kind of computer-printout blank verse, with side trips into Zen Japan—kept getting in the way. I think Doctorow is trying for a certain kind of irony, a saturnine, perhaps even prophetic, view of both the poor and rich in America, their intertwining and colliding destinies. But the balance goes awry.

> It could be that Doctorow shares too much with his hero, a certain over-respect for the super-rich; F. W. Bennett, a rather boring character, is written up as a wise and shaggy Buddha casting his spell everywhere. The plot becomes mechanistic, the characters puppets in a No play. A kind of Oriental stoicism may be part of the author's point. Philosophically, that is his right. But it robs the novel of real dramatic punch and what could have been considerable humanity.

You don't have to read past the first two words of this passage—"For me"—to recognize it as informal. But if you do read on, there's a long list of other informal characteristics. The expression "had its moments" (moments of what?) is colloquial; so are expressions like "getting in the way," "written up as," and "dramatic punch." The heavy use of the words "kind of" and the tendency to resort to zippy words ("super-rich") and metaphors ("a wise and shaggy Buddha") also identify this passage as informal.

Just for purposes of comparison, here's a more formal version of the same thing:

> Though *Loon Lake* is, at times, affecting, the mechanically poetic style, which partakes occasionally of a mysticism reminiscent of Japanese Zen philosophy, persistently interferes with one's enjoyment of the novel. Doctorow may be attempting to frame an ironic, saturnine, perhaps even

prophetic view of the intertwining and colliding destinies of the poor and rich in America; but the attempt does not succeed.

And so on. Here—again, just for purposes of comparison—is a passage from a formal essay on Doctorow by Geoffrey Galt Harpham, which originally appeared in the scholarly journal *PMLA:*

> In the mid-seventies Doctorow became increasingly intrigued by the concept of the interchangeability of parts and by the general idea of a technology of narrative. In *Loon Lake*, completed in 1979, he brings the technology up-to-date in a self-consciously state-of-the-art novel bearing the markings of the computer. The overt traces of the computer are most concentrated in intrusions on the narrative line—such as "Data comprising life F. W. Bennett undergoing review" (158), the annotations to Penfield's poems, the notes the author has written to himself ("I have a comment here. I note the boy Warren Penfield's relentless faculty of composition" [37–38])—and in the "reactions" of the program to itself ("Your register respectfully advises the need for additional countervailing data" [159]). Apart from these signatures, the faculty of the computer most frequently exploited by the author is its capacity to transpose information from one setting to another, the perfect mobility of its text. The computer liberates the writer from textual sequentiality, aug-

ments the writer's powers of repetition, and encourages a view of textual units—and the things they represent—as interchangeable.

Which one of these examples should you try to emulate? I'd say you should aim somewhere in between Sigal and Harpham. If Sigal's prose is a bit too breezy and chatty for an undergraduate paper, Harpham's is more than a bit too formal—and jargon-heavy. Your level of diction, of course, should vary with the kind of paper you're writing. A personal essay of the sort you might write for a composition class should tend toward informality; a research paper for a sociology class should tend toward formality.

One important thing to remember is that once you've decided upon an appropriate level of diction, *stick to it.* Many beginning writers inadvertently violate this rule, shifting in the middle of an essay from one level of diction to another without even realizing it. Here is an example of a sudden shift in level of diction:

> At great expense, I obtained the original manuscript of Professor Brogan's widely admired philosophical treatise, only to discover, alas, that it was really lousy.

The problem in this example is that "really lousy" is colloquial, while everything that precedes it is formal. To read such a sentence is to feel that the writer has suddenly changed into a different person—or, at least, that she is less certain than she should be of who she is. This is a very dangerous effect to create; any writer who sounds like William F. Buckley one minute and *Tiger Beat* magazine the next will probably not only confuse his readers but lose their confidence and respect as well. Sometimes it's one word, selected to impress, that throws off the level of diction:

> My sister bounded into the room, threw her shopping bags on the bed, and eagerly showed me all the new habiliments she had bought.
>
> My younger brother enjoyed consorting with me last weekend at my dormitory.

Habiliments and *consorting* are both lovely words, but in these sentences they are very much out of place. Reading these sentences, one doesn't concentrate upon the idea that they are attempting to communciate but upon those two words, which seem to have dropped in for a visit from other sentences in other essays. The writers of these sentences have clearly tried too hard; they've been dipping unnecessarily into the thesaurus, a tendency I like to refer to as *thesauritis*. In these cases there's absolutely nothing wrong with the simple, natural words—the ones that would come to mind first:

> My sister bounded into the room, threw her shopping bags on the bed, and eagerly showed me all the new clothes she had bought.

> My younger brother enjoyed spending time
> with me last weekend at my dormitory.

Sometimes an intentional shift in level of diction can be effective, usually for purposes of humor or irony:

> My sister bounded into the room, threw her shopping bags on the bed, and eagerly showed me all the new clothes she had bought. And a more costly collection of costumery you never saw.

Here the writer has emphasized the shift in level of diction by placing the fancy word *costumery* in a sentence that is itself highly informal (thanks to that "you never saw" expression, which is something of a colloquialism). The writer has also made use of alliteration—another device that is usually taboo in prose—for ironic effect.

At times, then, a shift in level of diction can be useful. But, unless you have a very clear reason for perpetrating such a shift, make every effort to keep your level of diction consistent throughout a given piece of writing.

◆

*Choose an appropriate level of
diction and maintain it.*

VI

Fine Points

40

Well begun is half done.
—Horace, *Epistles*

◆

Writing the Introduction

To many writers, the hardest part of an essay to write is the introduction. "I know what I want to say in the paper," runs an all-too-typical complaint, "but I just can't come up with an opening."

Ironically, one of the factors that make writing an introduction so challenging is the relative *freedom* that the introduction allows; there are, in other words, so many different possible ways of beginning almost any paper that writers can become immobilized by indecisiveness before they even begin.

Perhaps the most familiar method is the "funnel" method: start with a relatively broad generalization and, over the course of the introduction, narrow your focus until you arrive at your thesis. Barbara Braun uses this method in the introduction to her *Village Voice* article, "Cowboys and Indians: The History and Fate of the Museum of the American Indian":

> In this era of corporate raids and leveraged buyouts, the fate of small, undercapitalized cultural institutions mirrors that of their business counterparts. Where once museums seemed to occupy a niche apart from the mundane world, the current status of the Museum of the American Indian—also called the Heye Foundation—shows them subject to the same inexorable economic pressures. The fate of this fabulous repository of native artifacts, one of the world's largest collections of Indian material, hangs in the balance between takeover, merger, or other hazy alternatives, mainly because it lacks an adequate physical plant, financial basis, and a true consistency.

Braun begins by making a broad reference to current American economic trends ("In this era of corporate raids and leveraged buyouts . . ."). Immediately thereafter she narrows her field of discussion, indicating that her concern is not with the economic phenomena of "this era" as a whole but with "the fate of small, undercapitalized cultural institutions." Then she narrows even further, indicating that her particular interest, in this article, is the fate of the Museum of the American Indian. Braun's use of the "funnel" method accomplishes several things. Most importantly, perhaps, it serves to place her topic in context, establishing the fiscal crisis at the Museum of the American Indian not as an isolated problem but as a symptom of current financial trends—and therefore as a topic worth paying attention to even if one is not overly interested in Indian artifacts.

The "funnel" method, then, can be effective. But using the method thoughtlessly and habitually can yield highly ineffective results. Consider the following introduction to a paper about film comedian Robin Williams:

> In this troubled age of terrorism and nuclear proliferation, a couple of hours of entertainment can be a welcome escape from the horrors of reality. Movies are among America's favorite means of escape, and one of the most interesting movie actors of the present day is Robin Williams.

This introduction is inappropriate for several reasons. For one thing, the paragraph starts out *too* broadly; it's almost as if the writer is out to establish not his topic's importance but its relative triviality.

For another, the opening is misleading: the first few words seem to indicate that, whatever the topic turns out to be, it will have *something* to do with international politics.

There are several alternatives to the "funnel" method. One way is to begin with a relevant anecdote that attracts the interest of the reader. Such an anecdote may be autobiographical. Consider, for example, the opening sentences of the essay "Map of Israel, Map of Palestine," in which Meron Benvenisti introduces his topic—the conflict between the Israeli and Palestinian visions of their common homeland—by talking about his son:

> A little while ago, just before the Passover vacation, my son Yuval came home with the itinerary for his school outing. My father, who was there at the time, asked to see it. As he glanced through it, I could see something was making him angry. "Why are all the place names in Arabic?" he demanded. "Don't they know that these places have Hebrew names?"

Similarly, Gregg Easterbrook begins "What's Wrong with Congress?"—an essay in the *Atlantic Monthly* about confusion and disorder on Capitol Hill—with the following story:

> Representative Michael Synar, of Oklahoma, swears that this actually happened: He was addressing a Cub Scout Pack in Grove, Oklahoma, not far from his home

town of Muskogee. Synar asked the young boys if they could tell him the difference between the Cub Scouts and the United States Congress. One boy raised his hand and said, "We have adult supervision."

Another method is to begin with an example. In a review essay for the *New Yorker* entitled "The Warrior Prince," Alistair Cooke is principally concerned with describing the eccentric personality of the late Lord Mountbatten of Burma. He begins his essay, accordingly, with a striking illustration of that eccentricity:

> If ever you had cause to write to Lord Louis Mountbatten, the British Information Services in New York would be quick to warn you that while "Earl Mountbatten, Broadlands, Hampshire, England" would suffice, a letter so addressed would be painfully received by His Lordship. He expected the envelope to catalogue, in processional splendor, all his titles. The resulting two-line collection of honorifics might look like an elephantine joke to the writer but not to the addressee: Admiral of the Fleet, the Earl Mountbatten of Burma, K.G., P.C., G.C.B., O.M., G.C.S.I., G.C.I.E., G.C.V.O., D.S.O., F.R.S.

Yet another method is to begin by drawing a contrast. Consider the way James Atlas begins "A PEN Scrapbook" in *Vanity Fair*:

> The "extraordinary air of discontent" detected by Norman Mailer at the inaugural proceedings of the 48th International PEN Congress had vanished by the time the literary luminaries hit Saul Steinberg's thirty-four-room Park Avenue triplex for the opening-night bash.

Here Atlas contrasts the restive atmosphere of the congress itself with the relaxed atmosphere of the parties. Similarly, Martin Amis begins his *Vanity Fair* memoir of the poet Philip Larkin by contrasting Larkin's celebrity in Britain with his relative obscurity in America:

> Philip Larkin was not an inescapable presence in America, as he was in England, and to some extent you can see America's point. His Englishness was so desolate and inhospitable that even the English were often scandalized by it. Certainly, you won't find his work in the Personal Growth or Self-Improvement section of your local bookstore. "Man hands on misery to man," as he once put it:
>
>> It deepens like a coastal shelf.
>> Get out as early as you can,
>> And don't have any kids yourself.

Note how smoothly the contrast drawn in Amis's first sentence leads into his topic: Larkin's awesome negativity.

Many papers begin with a suggestion that the

person, place, object, condition, or concept under consideration is unique in some way or other. Randall Jarrell begins an essay about the war journalist Ernie Pyle by saying, "He wrote like none of the rest." Erica Jong begins a *New York Times Magazine* piece on Venice with the claim, "It is like no place on earth." Stephen Schwartz begins a *New Criterion* article on San Francisco literary life by differentiating San Francisco from other avant-garde intellectual centers:

> The San Francisco Bay Area has long enjoyed a reputation for experimental behavior on the part of its intellectuals—a confusion of art and life, if you will. But unlike Paris, Berlin, and Leningrad in the Twenties, or New York in the Forties, San Francisco has been much less a laboratory of the avant-garde than a cheering section.

A quotation is a good way to begin a paper—*if* it's relevant. Clive James begins "Unintelligibühl," an essay about the misuse of the English language on television, as follows:

> "If we ate what we listened to," said the pianist Earl Wild (BBC2), "we'd all be dead." He meant Muzak, but his observation applied equally well to the English language, which in this week's television received a fearful bashing from more than one direction.

Similarly, James begins an admiring essay about the prose of Raymond Chandler as follows:

> "In the long run," Raymond Chandler writes in *Raymond Chandler Speaking*, "however little you talk or even think about it, the most durable thing in writing is style, and style is the most valuable investment a writer can make with his time." At a time when literary values inflate and dissipate almost as fast as the currency, it still looks as if Chandler invested wisely. His style has lasted.

James's quotation is relevant, for his topic is Chandler's style; if his topic were something else—say, Chandler's plots or themes, or his ideas about American life—the quotation would be inappropriate.

Many a good introduction begins with one or more questions. Wilfred Sheed begins a *New York Times Book Review* essay called "The Writer as Something Else" as follows:

> Just to put a little suspense in this thing: What do you suppose the following people would have been if they hadn't been writers—Philip Roth, Jean Stafford, John Updike, Kurt Vonnegut, Murray Kempton, and Norman Mailer? Is there some shadow career that lopes alongside their prose and occasionally sticks its disappointed bloodhound face into their dreams?

As Sheed himself indicates, the purpose of beginning with a question or two is to create "a little suspense"—to pose a question that your readers may never have considered, but which, once posed, may intrigue them enough that they will want to read on and discover the answer.

Finally, sometimes the most effective way of beginning a paper is simply to state your thesis in a single brief sentence, thereupon proceeding directly into the body of the paper. "Our Greatest Invisible Actor," an essay about animator Chuck Jones that Lloyd Rose wrote for the *Atlantic*, begins as follows: "Chuck Jones is one of the great silent clowns of the screen, though he has only once appeared in front of the camera." That first sentence of the first paragraph is all Rose offers by way of introduction, and it's all that is needed.

An introduction, then, does not need to occupy an entire paragraph. In fact, the major problem with many—if not most—faulty introductions is that they are overelaborate: they take too long to get to the point. As for good introductions, though they come in all types, they share three predominant characteristics: they're interesting (if possible, arresting), they don't drag on for too long, and they lead smoothly and logically into the body of the paper.

◆

Make your introduction brief, engaging, and relevant.

41

It is easy to see the beginnings of things, and harder to see the ends.
—Joan Didion, *Slouching Towards Bethlehem*

◆

Writing the Conclusion

Quite often the problem with conclusions is this: you've finished saying what you had to say, you can't think of a blessed thing to add, but you can recognize that, as it stands, your paper concludes altogether too abruptly. You need, somehow, to tie together all the strands of your argument, need to strike precisely the right note at the end, need to leave your readers with your most vital points uppermost in their minds.

What, then, should you do? Here's what *not* to do: don't simply repeat your main points, one after the other, in more or less the same words you've already used. To do this is to risk boring your readers with unnecessary repetition. You may summarize what you have said, but try to do so as inventively and stylishly as you can. Though you *are* repeating yourself, try to make the repeated material sound as fresh as possible. And don't attract attention to the repetitiousness of your conclusion by beginning it with some expression like "To summarize what I have just demonstrated...." Your readers, who will probably feel that they *know* what you have just demonstrated, are likely to take this as a signal not to read any further. And you don't want that.

Nor, in your conclusion, should you bring up new topics, issues, questions, facts, or ideas; nor should you "broaden" your scope to a ridiculous degree; nor should you suddenly attempt to rise to new heights of eloquence and speak of your topic as if it were the most important and fascinating thing in the world. Keep your sense of perspective—as well as your tone, your point of view, and your level of diction. Don't feel as if you have to end every paper, as one does a day at Disneyland, with a fireworks display. Remember, you don't require an earthshaking topic in order to write an excellent paper; some of the best essays in history have been written on narrowly limited, seemingly inconsequential subjects.

And to suggest in a conclusion that your topic *is* more significant than it really is represents one of the surest ways of destroying a reader's confidence in your judgment and sense of proportion—and it is to do so, moreover, at that point in your paper when your reader's confidence in these things is most important of all.

Furthermore, whatever you do, don't undermine your paper by apologizing for what you've said or how you've said it, or by presenting facts or arguments that favor the opposing view. If you want to present such facts or arguments, do so in the body of the paper (and, wherever possible, contest those arguments). And don't pad your conclusion. If you can't think of much to say, then fine—don't say much. A conclusion doesn't have to be long or complicated. For instance, in an essay entitled "Terrorists and Spies" published in *The New Republic*, Walter Laqueur wraps up his discussion with three brief sentences:

> The intelligence reforms of the 1970s destroyed some controls and safeguards that were clearly needed. The pendulum was bound to swing back. But it took the Walker clan to prove the immense damage that can be done by even poorly paid amateurs, and to give the movement an impetus it otherwise might not have had.

You may not even need a concluding paragraph; instead, one or two good, solid concluding sentences at the end of your last paragraph may suffice.

But what, you ask, can you *say* in those final sentences? One answer: Look through your material. Is there a brief quotation from somebody or other that seems, in your view, to sum up the situation you're writing about? If so, perhaps you can focus your conclusion on that sentence. (Look through the body of your paper; perhaps there is a quotation there that you can lift out—without damaging the paper—and transplant into the conclusion.) Here, for example, is the concluding paragraph of an essay Richard N. Goodwin wrote for the *Los Angeles Times,* arguing that the United States should side with the black revolutionaries against the ruling white minority in South Africa:

> "Nothing is more certainly written in the book of fate," Jefferson wrote of American blacks, "than these people are to be free." Iran taught us the stupidity of association with an oppressive minority. In South Africa we still have a chance to be allied with the forces of future rule rather than with a crumbling tyranny. Nor is it just good fortune that moral imperatives and practical self-interest urge us in the same direction. Our values as a nation are the only compass that we have to guide us through the storm-stained continent of the emerging world.

The quotation from Jefferson gives this closing paragraph an elegance and authority that it would not otherwise have.

I have said that a conclusion should not bring

up new facts or ideas, and should not involve much broadening of scope. This is not to say, though, that you may not move slightly—but only *slightly*—beyond what you have said in the paper. You may ask yourself: "If I have fully explained or proved the thesis sentence, then what logically follows?" Your answer to this question will yield not a "new" idea but a logical and sensible extension of your discussion. If you've been discussing a political situation, a cultural phenomenon, or some such matter, you may wish in your conclusion to speculate about what the future will bring. In an essay entitled "Traveller in Albania," which describes the current political climate in that country, Paul Lendvai, writing in *Encounter*, concludes by moving from the present to the future, and wondering what will happen when Albania's present leader dies:

> Will a post-Hoxha Albania "thaw," and open itself to the world? A riddle, an enigma, a mystery. What is certain is that any Albanian leadership will be imbued with the same defiant spirit of solo and sudden turns, will remain a maverick in a changing world. Repeatedly in history Albania has played a significant role out of all proportion to its size, population, and resources. In view of its strategic position on the Adriatic, with the ethnic Albanians emerging as yet another "powder-keg" in Yugoslavian politics, and the recurring minority and border problems with Greece, major and (in the long

> run) inevitable changes in Albanian foreign and domestic policy are bound to affect the balance of power in the Balkans. Albania may be at the heart of "darkest Europe," but the Sons of the Eagle could alter the course of East-West confrontation.

While looking toward the future, Lendvai manages in this conclusion to summarize his main points without appearing to repeat himself. Instead of saying "In conclusion, Albania is a maverick nation with influence beyond its size, population, and resources; it is at the heart of 'darkest Europe,' occupies a strategic position on the Adriatic, and has troublesome relationships with Yugoslavia and Greece"—instead of writing this, Lendvai relegates most of the main points of his essay to subordinate clauses in his conclusion, reserving the main clauses for his brief glimpse into the future. By doing this, he manages to do two important things at once: one, he repeats the main points of the essay for subtle emphasis; and two, he breathes fresh air into the essay right up to the last words of the last sentence.

J. Hoberman, in the conclusion of an article on the movie director Rainer Werner Fassbinder for *American Film*, does much the same thing. He doesn't write, "To sum up, Fassbinder's films are notable primarily for their abrupt shifts in tone, magnification of individual gestures, fascination with human embarrassment, deliberate stylistic incongruities, free-floating irony, underlying pessimism, ruthless sociology, and continual threat of psychic disintegration." Such a conclusion would be dull, mechanical, utterly styleless. Instead of doing this, Hoberman (having mentioned, in his next-to-last paragraph, his recent viewing of Fassbinder's 1981 film *Lola*) writes:

> But beyond *Lola*'s specifics, the abrupt shift in tone, magnification of individual gestures, fascination with human embarrassment, deliberate stylistic incongruities, free-floating irony, underlying pessimism, ruthless sociology, and continual threat of psychic disintegration (here contained) mapped out a unique sensibility that I realized I had come to take for granted. I don't think I speak for myself alone in observing that the absence of this world view will be felt long before its subtleties are understood.

Like Lendvai, Hoberman manages here to sum up the main points of his essay—in this case, the components of Fassbinder's filmic vision—without seeming to be mired in repetition. His emphasis in this concluding paragraph is not on that list of characteristics but on the fact that these characteristics reflected a sensibility that he has only now begun to appreciate. Like Lendvai, he looks toward the future, speculating (very briefly) on Fassbinder's impact in the years to come.

The "look toward the future" is, in fact, a favorite concluding device. For example, in an essay entitled "William Empson: A Tribute," first published in *The New Criterion*, the distinguished literary critic Cleanth Brooks wraps up his discussion of his fellow critic's career as follows:

> I take it that his work is at the moment out of fashion. But then, the literary world is notoriously given to fads and fashions. What is of importance is the very solid achievement that he has left it. If the generations to come neglect that, they have impoverished none but themselves.

Brooks might simply have concluded his essay by saying: "To sum up, Empson achieved a lot." That, after all, is his basic point here. But to conclude his essay in such a blunt manner would have been dull and unimaginative. Brooks could have fleshed out the conclusion by overwriting; but that, too, would have been a mistake. Instead, he chooses to give life and substance to his conclusion by emphasizing not the past (Empson's career) but the future (Empson's legacy).

A similar concluding gambit is to discuss possible solutions to a problem that one has been describing. In the last paragraph of a *Los Angeles Times* essay on the supposed problem of devil worship in the songs of the rock group AC/DC, Robert Hilburn writes:

> The wisest thing we can do as parents is to maintain a dialogue with our children. The stronger a foundation youngsters have, the better they are equipped to deal with life's temptations. Just as today's parents made it past Elvis and the Stones with the

right support, so will today's kids make it past AC/DC.

Finally, a familiar approach to conclusions is to step back and take a slightly broader view—to place what you've been writing about in its cultural, historical, or sociological context. At the end of a detailed analysis of a newsmagazine program called *West 57th*, for instance, Tom Carson of *The Village Voice* argues that the program's superficial approach to serious news events is a characteristic phenomenon of the 1980s:

> *West 57th*'s comprehension of serious issues may only be the latest dramatization of the '80s dictum that when the means can justify themselves, the ends are pretty much beside the point, and most of us probably don't expect anything better than that. But the show's taste in whimsy may be beyond the power of even an audience raised on *Gidget* to endure.

Note here that Carson has also managed to turn a nice twist on an old cliché, "The ends justify the means." Such a twist is always an effective closing technique.

◆

Don't use your conclusion to introduce new topics or to make an exaggerated claim for the importance of your subject.

42

. . . forget the He and She.
—John Donne, *The Undertaking*

♦

"Sexist" Writing

"Every language," write Casey Miller and Kate Swift in the introduction to *The Handbook of Nonsexist Writing* (1980), "reflects the prejudices of the society in which it evolved." Along with many other feminists, Miller and Swift believe that the English language is full of terms, rules of usage, and grammatical constructions that demean women. They, and activists like them, have persuaded many writers to depart from many of the traditional rules of English and to adhere instead to newly formulated rules for "nonsexist writing." The influence of these new rules has been especially strong among college faculties—so strong, in fact, that many a sentence that would have been considered unobjectionable twenty years ago is now likely to be marked "SEXIST!" by a professor.

Many of the rules of nonsexist writing are amply justified. Miller and Swift argue for "parallel treatment" of men and women. If adult males are described in a piece of writing as "men," adult females should be described as "women," not "girls." The formulation "man and wife" should be avoided, and "husband and wife" used instead. Women should not be referred to by their first names when men are referred to by their last names. If a husband and wife are both physicians, they should not be identified as "Dr. and Mrs." but as "Drs." A businessman should not refer to his female secretary as "my girl." Such rules make sense and do no harm to the language.

Many writers and editors, however, feel that the movement for nonsexist language has had some unfortunate consequences. Perhaps the most controversial of these consequences is the widespread objection, among advocates of nonsexist writing, to the use of the pronouns *he*, *him*, *his*, and *himself* when the sex of the singular antecedent is unspecified. A few years ago, a sentence such as the following would have been considered grammatically correct:

> *Every* reader bases *his* first impression of a piece of writing upon its physical appearance.

But many professors nowadays would mark this sentence wrong. The *his*, they insist, is sexist, and should be replaced either by *his or her* or *his/her*. Some professors even encourage the treatment of words like *each, every, everyone,* and *everything* as plurals:

> Every reader bases their first impression of a piece of writing upon its physical appearance.

But many writers and editors object to these alternatives. They sincerely feel that the extensive use of "he or she," "him or her," "his or her," and "himself or herself" is awkward, that the formulations *he/she, him/her, his/her,* and *himself/herself* are unattractive, and that the use of *they, them, their,* and *themselves* as singular pronouns is ungrammatical. Some of these writers and editors feel, furthermore, that the use of *he* to refer to a person of unspecified sex is not at all sexist but is, rather, simply an instance of a single pronoun form having two distinct grammatical functions—a common enough linguistic occurrence. But many advocates of "nonsexist writing" have little respect for these views, and are likely to accuse the people that hold them of sexism.

Most of the time, the controversial *he* can be avoided by changing singular constructions to plural constructions. The sentence quoted above, for example, can be altered as follows:

> *All* readers base *their* first impressions of a piece of writing upon its physical appearance.

Every so often, however, you may be confronted by a sentence in which an alteration would result in unacceptable awkwardness or confusion. In such an instance, unless you can rewrite the sentence entirely, you may be forced to choose between following the traditional rule (thereby offending many proponents of nonsexist writing) and following the nonsexist rule (thereby offending many adovcates of grammatical propriety and stylistic grace). The best advice is to know your audience's preferences, and act accordingly. If your own convictions are strong and are contrary to your audience's, be prepared for the consequences.

◆

In the matter of "sexist" writing, consider your audience's preferences.

43

Fain would I dwell on form. . . .
—William Shakespeare, *Romeo and Juliet*

◆

Proper Manuscript Form

Manuscript form is not the most important thing in the world. The way a paper is written is far more important than the way it is typed. Still, proper manuscript form can make a great deal of difference in the way a reader perceives a piece of writing. All readers base their first impressions of a piece of writing upon its physical appearance—the kind of paper it's typed on, the way the pages are bound, the adherence (or lack thereof) to the rules of form, the presence (or absence) of cross-outs and sloppy typographical errors, and so forth. Well-ordered papers, to most readers, look like the work of well-ordered minds. Conversely, sloppy papers look like the work of sloppy minds. Of course, it is wrong to draw connections between the neatness of a paper and the quality of its ideas or its prose; after all, a perfectly typed manuscript may be poorly written and a poorly typed manuscript may be brilliantly written. Yet, consciously or unconsciously, this is the way most people form their initial impressions whenever they sit down to read a manuscript. It is to every writer's advantage to remember this and to respond accordingly. Writers should remember, also, that first impressions have a way of lingering in the mind. And so many teachers, whether they realize it or not, may, when faced with two papers of equal merit, award a higher grade to the one that *looks* nicer. It happens all the time.

So, when you're preparing to hand in a paper, it's only good sense to make it as presentable as possible. Having labored so hard at crystallizing your ideas in words, why offer them to your teacher in a form that is unworthy of the effort?

Always follow your teacher's instructions regarding manuscript form. If there are none, observe the following suggestions. Every paper should be typed, double spaced, on white paper that measures eight and one-half by eleven inches. The type should be dark and clear and easy to read. Don't use old, faded ribbons, fancy type faces, dot-matrix printing, or erasable paper; they all make a paper harder to read. Don't use colored paper or colored ribbons; they look unprofessional. Don't bind your paper with staples or by using the double-fold-and-rip method, and don't use plastic binders; the most professional way to bind a paper is with a simple paper clip. Type only on one side of each sheet and leave one-inch margins at the top and bottom and on both sides. On all pages, except the first, put the page number in the upper right-hand corner of the page—not at the very edge of the paper, but an inch from the top and an inch from the right; the first line of text should be four spaces below the page number. It's a good idea to put your name on every page, preceding the page number (e.g., "Smith - 5"), just in case the pages get mixed up or come loose.

The upper right-hand corner of the title page should carry your name, the name of the course and professor, and the date—all double spaced, as follows:

> Christie Brinkley
> ANT 101
> Professor Kim Stewart
> January 22, 1987

The title of the paper should appear in the center of the page, two spaces below the date. Do *not* underline the title or put all the words in uppercase letters or use quotation marks. Of course, if the title contains words that should be underlined, put in uppercase letters, or placed within quotation marks, then by all means do what is required:

> Friendship and Love in *The Folded Leaf*
>
> The Ending of Dorothy Parker's "Big Blonde"
>
> The Founding of UNICEF

Don't follow the title with a period.

If you are writing a research paper, you will have to provide notes and a bibliography. Unless your teacher expresses a preference, the *notes* may be either footnotes (which appear at the bottom of the page) or endnotes (which appear together at the end of the paper). Research papers are based on the accumulation of facts, and the purpose of notes is to tell your reader where you got those facts. Well-known facts don't have to be noted. If you mention in your paper that Rome is the capital of Italy, for instance, there's no need for a note.

The form that a note takes depends on the type of source you are citing. If you are citing a book, the note should look like this:

> [1]Jay McInerney, *Ransom* (New York: Vintage, 1985), p. 25.

Note that the author's first name precedes his last name; the book's title is italicized (underlined); the city of publication, the publishing house, and the year of publication are placed within parentheses; and the word *page* is abbreviated. (*Pages* is abbreviated pp.)

If a book has two or three authors, list all of them:

> [2]Casey Miller and Kate Swift, *The Handbook of Nonsexist Writing* (New York: Lippincott & Crowell, 1980), p. 22.

If there are more than three authors, give only the name of the first of them, and follow it with the Latin words *et al.* (there is a period following the "al."). If the edition you are citing is not the first edition, indicate which edition it is:

> [3]Robert S. Ross, *American National Government*, 3rd ed. (Boston: Houghton Mifflin, 1981), p. 32.

If the book does not have an author but has an editor, name that person and indicate that he or she is the editor:

> [4]Harry M. Geduld, ed., *Focus on D. W. Griffith* (Englewood Cliffs, N.J.: Prentice-Hall, 1971), p. 12.

If you are citing an article, story, or poem contained within such a book, however, the author and his work should be named first:

> [5]G. Charles Niemeyer, "David Wark Griffith," in *Focus on D. W. Griffith*,

ed. Harry M. Geduld (Englewood Cliffs, N.J.: Prentice-Hall, 1971), p. 134.

If you are citing something that has been translated, both the author and translator should be named, as follows:

[6]Charles Baudelaire, "The Swan," trans. F. P. Sturm, in Edward Engelberg, ed., *The Symbolist Poem* (New York: Dutton, 1967), p. 131.

And if you are citing a book with several volumes, indicate with a roman numeral which volume you are quoting from:

[7]Wallace I. Matson, *A New History of Philosophy,* II (San Diego: Harcourt Brace Jovanovich, 1986), p. 381.

If you're citing an article or story from a weekly magazine, the citation should look like this:

[8]Lance Morrow, "The Start of a Plague Mentality," *Time,* 23 September 1985, p. 92.

This issue of *Time* is Volume 126, Number 12, but this information should not be used in the footnote. Nor do you have to write the date this way (you could write September 23, 1985), but it *is* easier to read.

If you're citing a newspaper article, mention which section the article is in and the column number from which you are quoting:

> [9]Morgan Gendel, "Cosby & Co.: What Makes the Show a Hit?" *Los Angeles Times*, 26 September 1985, Calendar section, p. 1, col. 2.

If you're quoting from a journal, you should find out whether the pages of the journal are numbered consecutively throughout an entire year's worth of issues or whether each issue begins with a new page one. If the former is the case, then it is not necessary to give the issue number and date; just give the volume and year:

> [10]Roger Pooley, "Berryman's Last Poems: Plain Style and Christian Style," *Modern Language Review*, 76 (1981), 291.

If the latter is the case, then the issue number and date should be given:

> [11]John Colville, "How the West Lost the Peace in 1945," *Commentary*, 80:3 (September 1985), 46.

The numbers indicate that this is Volume 80, Number 3. Note that the letter *p* doesn't appear before the page number in either of the preceding examples; this is the recommended practice when the volume number of a periodical is given.

A book review should be cited as follows:

> [12]Jeffrey Marsh, "Brave New World," rev. of *The 2025 Report*, by Norman Macrae, *Commentary*, 80:3 (September 1985), 76.

When citing encyclopedia or almanac articles, don't give volume or page numbers if the articles appear in alphabetical order and are one page or less in length. If the articles are not alphabetized or are more than a page long, the page number *is* required.

A dissertation is cited as follows:

> [13]Patricia Ann Brenner, "John Berryman's *Dream Songs:* Manner and Matter." Diss. Kent State University 1970, p. 125.

Later citations from the same source may be abbreviated. Simply use the author's name:

> [14]Brenner, p. 180.

If you have cited two works by the same author, include a shortened form of the title in your subsequent references:

> [15]Marsh, "Brave," p. 77.

If you have cited works by two authors with the same last name, use the full name of the author in your subsequent references:

> [16]Jeffrey Marsh, p. 77.

A *bibliography*, which comes at the end of a paper and should include the names of all works used in its preparation, calls for citations of a different form. A book, for instance, should be cited as follows:

> McInerney, Jay. *Ransom*. New York: Vintage, 1985.

Note that the author's last name precedes his first name, that periods are used to separate author from title and title from publication data, and that no page numbers appear.

When a book has two or three authors, only the name of the first should be given last name first:

> Reisz, Karel and Gavin Millar. *The Technique of Film Editing*. New York: Focal Press, 1968.

Note that when a bibliographical entry runs more than one line, the subsequent lines are indented. (With notes, whether footnotes or endnotes, the opposite is the case: the first line, and only the first line, of a note is indented.) If a book has more than three authors, the Latin words *et al.* should be used, as in a note.

If a book has an editor, it should be cited as follows:

> Geduld, Harry M., ed. *Focus on D. W. Griffith*. Englewood Cliffs, N.J.: Prentice-Hall, 1971.

An article, story, or poem in such a book should be cited in this way:

> Niemeyer, G. Charles. "David Wark Griffith." In *Focus on D. W. Griffith*.

> Ed. Harry M. Geduld. Englewood Cliffs, N.J.: Prentice-Hall, 1971.

The citation of a translated work should be written in this manner:

> Baudelaire, Charles. "The Swan." Trans. F. P. Sturm. In *The Symbolist Poem.* Ed. Edward Engelberg. New York: Dutton, 1967.

A book in several volumes should be cited as follows:

> Matson, Wallace I. *A New History of Philosophy.* 2 vols. San Diego: Harcourt Brace Jovanovich, 1986.

A newspaper article citation should take the following form:

> Gendel, Morgan. "Cosby & Co.: What Makes the Show a Hit?" *Los Angeles Times,* 26 September 1985, Calendar section, p. 1, cols. 1–4, and p. 10, cols. 4–6.

Observe that whereas the note for this article mentions only the column where the note quotation is found, the bibliographical citation gives the page-and-column information for the entire article. A magazine article citation should look like this:

> Morrow, Lance. "The Start of a Plague Mentality." *Time.* 23 September 1985, p. 92.

The article appears *only* on page 92.

An article from a journal with consecutive pagination throughout the volume should be cited as follows:

> Pooley, Roger. "Berryman's Last Poems: Plain Style and Christian Style." *Modern Language Review*, 76 (1981), 291–97.

An article from a journal with separate pagination for each issue should be cited in this way:

> Colville, John. "How the West Lost the Peace in 1945." *Commentary*, 80:3 (September 1985), 41–47.

A book review should be cited in this way:

> Marsh, Jeffrey. "Brave New World." Rev. of *The 2025 Report*, by Norman Macrae. *Commentary*, 80:3 (September 1985), 76–77.

A dissertation is cited thus:

> Brenner, Patricia Ann. "John Berryman's *Dream Songs:* Manner and Matter." Diss. Kent State University 1970.

If you cite more than one work by the same author, rather than repeating the author's name, use ten hyphens followed by a period:

Epstein, Joseph. "Max Beerbohm." *The New Criterion*, 4:1 (September 1985), 22–33.

----------. "One Cheer for E. M. Forster." *Commentary*, 80:3 (September 1985), 48–57.

◆

Follow standard guidelines for manuscript preparation.

44

Usage, in whose hands lies the judgment, the right and the rule of speech.
—Horace, *Ars Poetica*

◆

Usage

There are tens of thousands of words in the English language. Of this number, a generous handful seem to cause more problems than all the others put together. Writers often misspell these words, or confuse one with another, or misconstrue their meanings. The word **usage** itself is on the list of problem words. Many writers apparently think of it as a sophisticated way of saying *use*, whereas actually the two words have quite different meanings. Perhaps the most familiar—and therefore most vexing—of all usage errors in American English is the writing of the two words *a lot* as one word. *A lot* is two words. Second most familiar, perhaps, is *alright*, a common misspelling of *all right*.

Herewith, a glossary of usage:

a, an Use *a* before words that begin with consonant sounds, whether or not they actually begin with consonants (*a rutabaga, a eucalyptus tree*); use *an* before words that begin with vowel sounds, whether or not they begin with vowels (*an eternity, an hour*).

a lot, alot Always two words: *a lot*.

accept, except *Accept* is a verb meaning "to receive," as in "Will you *accept* this gift?" *Except* can be a verb, meaning "to exclude" (as in "Congress *excepted* Indians living on reservations from the obligation to pay federal taxes"), but it is usually a preposition meaning "other than" or "but": "I will *accept* all these gifts, *except* for the pet lobster from Uncle Mike."

adverse, averse *Adverse* means "harmful"; *averse* means "opposed." "I am *averse* to Communism because it has an *adverse* effect upon human liberties."

advice, advise *Advice* is the noun, *advise* is the verb. When you *advise* people, you give them *advice*.

affect, effect In their most common meanings, *affect* is the verb, *effect* is the noun. When you *affect* something, you have an *effect* upon it. *Effect* can also be a verb meaning "to bring about": "The election of Franklin Roosevelt *effected* a great change in American government." And *affect* can also be a noun (used mostly by psychologists) meaning "emotion."

aggravate *Aggravate* is often used in conversation to mean "irritate": "Jim's singing aggravated me." But in writing, it should be used only to mean "intensify, worsen": "The noise of the construction crew outside bothered me, and Jim's singing *aggravated* the situation still further."

agree to, agree with To *agree to* is to consent to; to *agree with* is to share an opinion with. "Jasmine *agreed with* me that it was unfair of her parents not to *agree to* our marriage."

all, all of *All* is usually sufficient; the exception is when the next word is a personal pronoun: "Not *all of* us believe that *all* truth is relative."

all ready, already There are, of course, two words *all* and *ready* that can be used together, but the term meaning "by now" is spelled as one word (with one *l*): *already*. "It's *already* after eight o'clock, and still the women are not *all ready* to go to the party."

all right, alright The preferred spelling is *all right:* "It's *all right* with me if we miss the beginning of the party."

all together, altogether Again, there are two words *all* and *together*, but the term meaning "entirely" is spelled as one word (with one *l*): *altogether*. "At the party, the members of the swim team were *all together* in one corner of the room, and they looked *altogether* depressed over their recent loss to UCLA."

allude to, refer to To *allude to* something is to mention it indirectly; to *refer to* it is to mention it directly.

among, between *Among* usually refers to more than two people or things, and *between* refers to two.

amount, number Use *number*, not *amount*, to refer to things that can be counted. "Dave came home from the party with a small *amount* of ice cream and a large *number* of cookies."

and etc. Since *et cetera* means "and so forth," the expression *and etc.* is redundant. Just write *etc.* Never use the symbol & or + for *and*, unless such a symbol is part of a name or title or appears in a quotation.

anyway, anyways, any way The two words *any* and *way* can be used together, but the word meaning "in any case" is one word: *anyway*. *Anyways* is colloquial and should be avoided in writing. "There isn't *any way* to get to Richmond before sundown, but I'm going to try to do it *anyway*."

as . . . as, so . . . as When making a positive comparison, use the word *as* twice; when making a negative comparison, you may use *as* twice or *so* and *as*, though the latter is preferred. "I love you *as* much *as* I did yesterday, but not *so* much *as* I will tomorrow."

assure, ensure, insure To *assure* is to promise, to *ensure* or *insure* is to make certain. But many writers like to use only *ensure* to mean "make certain" and to use *insure* to mean "take out an insurance policy." "I *assured* Kris that *insuring* her car would *ensure* her financial solvency."

awhile, a while *A while* is composed of an article and a noun, so the term can be used as follows: "Mr. Swenson has been in town for *a while*." *Awhile* is an adverb: "Mr. Swenson has been in town *awhile*."

bad, badly *Bad* is an adjective, *badly* an adverb. But *bad* is ordinarily used with verbs like "to feel," with "feel" acting as a linking verb: "I feel *bad*." Do not say "I feel *badly*."

being that, being as These are unacceptable ways of saying "because" or "since." Just say "because" or "since."

beside, besides *Beside* means "next to," *besides* means "in addition to." "You'll be safe if you stand *beside* me; *besides*, you'll be warmer that way."

bring, take Don't use these words interchangeably. To *bring* something is to carry it closer; to *take* something is to carry it farther away. "*Take* this album home with you and *bring* it back to me when you're finished."

can, may *Can* indicates ability, *may* indicates permission. "I *can* drive a car, but the law says I *may* not do so in this state until I'm seventeen."

censor, censure, censer, sensor To *censor* is to prohibit the dissemination of books, movies, and the like, or to cut parts out of them; this is the job of a person called a *censor*. To *censure* is to criticize severely, and such severe criticism is called *censure*. "The network president *censured* the *censor* for *censoring* the late-night comedy program." A *censer* is a container, used in religious rituals, in which incense is burned. And a *sensor* is an instrument designed to respond to a specific stimulus.

continual, continuous *Continual* means "recurring with interruptions," *continuous* means "uninterrupted." "The *continuous* sound of the surf was *continually* punctuated by the sound of foghorns."

convince, persuade You *convince* someone of an opinion and *persuade* someone to do something. "Once we had *convinced* Gary that the cause was a good one, we were able to *persuade* him to donate some money."

could of This should be *could have* (or, colloquially, *could've*).

criteria This is the plural of *criterion*.

data This is the plural of a seldom-used word, *datum*.

device, devise *Device* is the noun, *devise* the verb. "Nancy *devised* a *device* for collecting data."

differ from, differ with To *differ with* is to disagree with; to *differ from* is to be different from. "Sue and I *differ from* each other in our ancestry and *differ with* each other politically."

different from, different than *Different from* is always correct; *different than* should be used only when it saves words: "My first rock concert was *different than* I had expected." (The alternative, one word longer, is: "My first rock concert was *different from* what I had expected.")

discreet, discrete *Discreet* means "prudent," *discrete* means "separate and distinct."

disinterested, uninterested *Disinterested* means "impartial"; *uninterested* means "not interested."

Due to This term is acceptable after a form of the verb "to be." "John's election loss was due to the revelation that he had murdered a family in Nebraska." But don't use *due to* to begin a sentence: "Due to the revelation that John had murdered a family in Nebraska, he lost the election." Use "Because of" or "As a result of."

each and every Redundant. Use one word or the other.

e.g., i.e. Don't confuse these two terms: *e.g.* (from

the Latin *exempli gratia*) means "for example"; *i.e.* (*id est*) means "that is."

eminent, immanent, imminent *Eminent* means "famous"; *immanent* means "inherent"; *imminent* means "about to happen."

enthused A form of the verb "to enthuse," meaning "to be enthusiastic" or "to make enthusiastic." "He *enthused* over the beauty of the countryside." But the word's most common use, as an adjective, is colloquial: "He was so *enthused* about the beauty of the countryside." Use *enthusiastic* instead.

equally as Ungrammatical. The word "as" is sufficient.

especially, specially *Especially* means "particularly"; *specially* means "specifically."

exact same Don't use this term; instead write "exactly the same."

[the] fact that This expression is usually unnecessary. "*The fact that* Don ate lunch with Elsa is inconsequential." This can be shortened to "*That* Don ate lunch with Elsa is inconsequential." Also: "I am impressed by *the fact that* you wrote a whole book." This can be shortened to "I am impressed that you wrote a whole book."

farther, further *Further* can be used in any sense; *farther* should be used only in regard to measurable distance. "The scientists made *further* explorations to determine why the satellite had traveled *farther* than expected."

fewer, less *Fewer* refers to number, *less* to amount. "There were *fewer* people at the meeting, and therefore *less* discussion than usual."

flaunt, flout To *flaunt* is to show off, to *flout* is to defy. "He *flouted* the rules of good taste by *flaunting* his wealth."

former, latter If the sentence is relatively uncomplicated, and if there are only two items listed, then you can use *former* to refer to the first item and *latter* to refer to the second. "Today I ate French toast and steak—the *former* for breakfast, the *latter* for supper." But with more than two items, don't use *former* or *latter:* "Today I ate French toast, a bowl of soup, and steak—the first for breakfast, the second for lunch, the third for supper."

good, well *Good* is an adjective, *well* an adverb. "Mark drives *well*; he's a *good* driver." *Well* is also an adjective meaning "healthy." "As soon as Mark is *well*, we can go driving again."

had better This is an acceptable construction. Don't use "better" instead. "You better not pout" should be "You *had better* not pout" (or "You'd better not pout").

hanged, hung A person dangling from a rope has been *hanged*; everything else suspended from a rope, a hook, or what-have-you is *hung*. "Before he was *hanged*, the murderer *hung* a photograph of Marlo Thomas in his cell."

illusion, allusion, delusion An *allusion* is a reference to something, an *illusion* is a deceptive appearance, a *delusion* is a fantastic belief. "Dave's *allusion* to Ibsen's plays gave the *illusion* that he was a literary scholar; Sue says he suffers under the *delusion* that he is T. S. Eliot."

imply, infer To *imply* is to suggest indirectly; to *infer* is to conclude. "By giving Andrew a cookbook, Scott *implied* that he was a bad cook; or at least that was what Andrew *inferred* from the look on Scott's face."

it's, its *It's* is a contraction meaning "it is"; *its* is a possessive pronoun. "*It's* strange to watch a snake shed *its* skin."

lay, lie *Lay* means "put"; the past tense is "laid" and the present participle is "have laid." *Lie* means "recline"; its past tense is "lay" and its present participle is "have lain." "Millicent said, '*Lay* that book down on the table, then *lie* down and get some rest.' So I *laid* the book down on the table and *lay* down to get some rest."

lead, led *Lead* (pronounced "leed") is the present tense, *led* is the past tense. *Lead* (pronounced "led") is also the name of a metallic element.

lend, loan *Lend* is a verb, *loan* a noun. "If I ask Skip for a *loan* of fifty dollars, do you think he'll *lend* it to me?" (*Loan* can also be a verb, but *lend* is preferable.)

like, as *Like* is a preposition, *as* a conjunction. So if you are connecting two clauses, use *as*, not *like*. You can say "This tastes *like* beer," but you can't say "This tastes refreshing, like a beer should." Similarly, "He looked at us *like* we were crazy" should be "He looked at us *as if* we were crazy." *As* can also be a preposition: "She served *as* a waitress." (Notice the difference between this and the sentence "She served *like* a waitress.")

literally This means "actually." But it is often used incorrectly to mean "figuratively": "I *literally* went through the roof when I got the electricity bill." Use *literally* only when you are presenting the straight truth: "I *literally* spent one-hundred dollars on clothing today."

loose, lose *Loose* is an adjective meaning "not tight"; *lose* is a verb meaning "mislay" or "suffer a loss." "If you don't do something about that *loose* tie line, you're going to *lose* your boat."

mad This should be used only as a synonym for "insane," not "angry."

may be, maybe *May be* is a verb phrase; *maybe* is an adjective meaning "perhaps." "I *may be* going to Acapulco this summer, but *maybe* I'll go to Mazatlán instead."

media This is the much-overused plural of the word *medium*. Don't use it as a synonym for "television."

moral, morale A *moral* is a lesson drawn from an event or a story; *morale* is a state of mind. *Moral*, as an adjective, means "ethical." "Ever since Roberta's adolescent *moral* behavior has been drawn into question, her *morale* has been frighteningly low—the *moral* of which is, you can't escape your past."

must of Should be "must have."

no one Always two words.

nor *Nor* should be used only as the second half of the correlative conjunction *neither . . . nor* or to introduce a main clause after a negative main clause. "I don't need a new shirt nor a tie" should therefore be "I don't need a new shirt or a tie." (The words "a tie" are *not* a clause.) But "I don't need a new shirt, nor do I need a tie" is correct. (The words "do I need a tie" *are* a clause.)

precede, proceed To *precede* is to come before, to *proceed* is to go forward. "When he heard that David had *preceded* him in Tammy's affections, he *proceeded* to sharpen his Bowie knife."

principal, principle As a noun, *principal* refers to an official (such as the head of a school) or a sum of money; as an adjective, it means "main." *Principle* is a noun meaning "rule." "My school *principal* told me his life is ruled by a simple *principle:* Do unto others before they do unto you."

provided, provided that, providing All three are correct.

quote *Quote* is a verb; the noun is *quotation*.

raise, rise To *raise* is to lift something, to *rise* is to get up. "*Rise* from the table and *raise* your glass in a toast."

real, really *Real* is an adjective, *really* an adverb. "Your apartment is *really* attractive." (Not *real*.)

reason is because Don't use the words *reason* and *because* together. Write either "My *reason* for dropping by is that I'm hungry" or "I'm dropping by *because* I'm hungry."

sometime, sometimes, some time *Sometime* refers to an unspecified time in the future, and can also mean "former"; *sometimes* means "now and then"; *some time* means "a period of time." "*Sometimes* I hope that Penny, my *sometime* girlfriend, will come to New York *sometime* and spend *some time* with me."

stationary, stationery *Stationary* means "standing still," *stationery* is writing paper.

supposed to Don't make the mistake of writing this as *suppose to*.

than, then *Than* is a conjunction used in comparisons: "I am taller *than* you." *Then* is an adverb indicating time or cause-and-effect relationships: "If you're taller, *then* I'll pay you ten dollars."

that, which *That* introduces restrictive clauses—clauses, that is, which are necessary to the meaning of the sentence: "Here's the book *that* I just bought." (Without the clause following *that*, we wouldn't know which book was being referred to.) *Which* can introduce restrictive clauses, but some writers reserve it for introducing nonrestrictive clauses—those that are not necessary to the meaning of the sentence: "Here's my new book, *which* I bought for seventeen dollars." (The clause following *which* isn't necessary to establish what book is being referred to; it merely offers additional information about the book.)

there, their, they're *Their* is the possessive form of "they"; *they're* is a contraction of "they are"; *there* is variously a noun, pronoun, adjective, or adverb with a number of uses and meanings. "If you're looking for Steve and Brian, *they're* over *there* in *their* car."

till, until, 'til *Till* and *until* are both correct, *'til* is not.

to, too, two *To* is a preposition that serves as the opposite of "from" and accompanies the infinitive form of a verb; *too* is an adverb meaning "also" or "excessively"; *two* is a number. "It's *too* cold for the *two* of us *to* go *to* the beach. And it's awfully late, *too*."

toward, towards Although either form is correct, *toward* is preferred.

unique To say that something is *unique* is to say that it is the only one of its kind. Uniqueness is not a matter of degree. Either you're unique or you're not; it makes no more sense to say "very unique" than to say "very dead." If you must use the word "very," say "very special" or "very unusual" or something of that sort.

usage, use, utilize   *Usage* is a noun meaning "habitual or customary practice," and is most often used to refer to the customs and conventions of a language. It is not a synonym for *use*. *Utilize* is a synonym for *use*, more or less, but is almost never necessary and nearly always pretentious.

used to   Don't make the mistake of writing *use to*.

were, where   *Were* is the plural, past-tense form of the verb "to be"; *where* is a word indicating location. "Where were you when I needed you?"

who, whom   *Whom* is not a "fancy" form of the word *who*. Whereas *who* should be used in the subjective case (that is, when it is the subject of a verb or stands for the subject), *whom* should be used in the objective case (when it is the object of a verb or stands for the object). "There go the men *who* burglarized my apartment": this sentence is correct because *who* stands for *men*, the subject of the verb *burglarized*. (It's the subject because these men performed the burglary.) "And there goes the man *whom* they mugged on the way up": this sentence is correct because *whom* stands for *man*, the object of the verb *mugged*. (It's the object because this man did not perform the mugging; he was the recipient of the action.)

whose, who's *Who's* is a contraction of "who is" or "who has"; *whose* is a possessive pronoun meaning "belonging to whom." *"Who's* going to tell me *whose* book this is, and *who's* been reading it?"

would of Should be *would have*.

your, you're *Your* is a possessive pronoun meaning "belonging to you"; *you're* is a contraction of "you are." *"You're* crazy to give *your* book away to him."

◆

Know the differences in meaning between often-confused words.

Index

A, an, 310
A lot, alot, 310
Abbreviation, 176–78
Abstract words, defined, 255
Accept, except, 310
Acronyms, 145
Active voice, 85–87
Adjective, defined, 71
Adverb, defined, 71
Adverse, averse, 310
Advice, advise, 310
Affect, effect, 311
Aggravate, 311
Agree to, agree with, 311
Agreement
  in gender, 108
  in number, 107–108
  in person, 108
  pronoun-antecedent, 107–110
  subject-verb, 96–110
All, all of, 311
All ready, already, 311
All right, alright, 311
All together, altogether, 312
Alliteration, 213–14
Allude to, refer to, 312
Allusion, delusion, illusion, 318
Among, between, 312

Amount, number, 312
And etc., 312
Antecedent, defined, 107
Anyway, anyways, any way, 312
Apostrophe, 129–34
  to indicate possession, 129–31
  to indicate an omission, 132
  misuse, 132–33
  used in some plurals, 133–34
Argumentative essay, 12
Article, defined, 71
As, like, 319
As . . . as, so . . . as, 312
Assonance, 213–14
Assure, ensure, insure, 313
Auxiliary verbs, defined, 70
Averse, adverse, 310
Awhile, a while, 313

Bad, badly, 313
Being that, being as, 313
Beside, besides, 313
Between, among, 312
Bibliography, 304–308
Both/and, 228
Brackets, 157–58
Bring, take, 313

325

Index

Can, may, 314
Capitals, 171–75
  abbreviations, 173
  first word of sentence, 174–75
  proper names, 171–72
  titles, 173–74
Cause and effect
  development by, 36–40
  organization by, 21
Censor, censure, censer, sensor, 314
Classification
  development by, 36–40
  organization by, 20
Clause, 76
  dependent, 77
  independent, 77
  non-restrictive, 116–17
  restrictive, 117
Clichés, 195–99
Coherence, defined, 49
Coherence, achieving
  by use of pronouns, 50–51
  by use of repetition, 49
  by use of synonyms, 51–53
  by use of transitional expressions, 53–58
Collective nouns, 102
Colloquial words, 265
Colon, 149–52
  to introduce a quotation, 151
  misuse, 151
  to set off independent clause, 149–50
Comma, 113–23
  between clauses, 115
  in comma splice, 93
  with dates, 120
  after introductory clause or phrase, 114
  after introductory transitional expressions, 115–16
  misuse, 120–23, 154
  with names and titles, 120
  to separate coordinate adjectives, 119
  to separate items in series, 117–18
  to set off parenthetical elements, 116
  with speaker tags, 120
Comma splice, 93–94
Comparison and contrast
  at beginning of paragraph, 47
  development by, 36, 40–41, 47
  organization by, 21–24
Complex sentence, 77
Compound-complex sentence, 79
Compound sentence, 76–77
Conclusion, 284–92
Concrete words, defined, 255

Conditional perfect tense, 69
Conditional tense, 69
Conjunction, defined, 72–73
   coordinating, 76, 225
   correlative, 228
   subordinating, 77
Connotation, 264
Continual, continuous, 314
Convince, persuade, 314
Coordinating conjunction, 76, 225
   repairing comma splice, 94
   repairing fused sentence, 95
Correlative conjunction, 228
Could of, 314
Criteria, 314

Dangling modifier, 83
Dash, 153–56
   for emphasis, 155
   excessive use of, 155
   to set off appositive, 156
   to set off independent clause, 156
Data, 315
Definition
   development by, 36
   organization by, 21
Delusion, allusion, illusion, 318
Dependent clause, 77

Description
   development by, 36, 41–42
   organization by, 21
Descriptive essay, 12
Development strategies, 35–43
   cause and effect, 36
   classification, 36–40
   comparison and contrast, 36, 40–41, 47
   definition, 36
   description, 36, 41–42
   example, 36–37, 40
   narration, 36, 41
   process analysis, 36
   repetition, 38–39
Device, devise, 315
Dialogue format, 138–39
Diction, appropriate level of, 263–72
Differ from, differ with, 315
Different from, different than, 315
Direct questions, 145–46
Discreet, discrete, 315
Disinterested, uninterested, 315
Due to, 315

E.g., 315–16
Each and every, 315
Effect, affect, 311
Either/or, 228
Ellipsis, 160–61

Eminent, immanent, imminent, 316
Emphasis, 216–24
   active voice, 223
   dash, 220–21
   exclamation point, 222
   italics, 222
   periodic sentence, 219–20
   punctuation, 155, 218
   repetition, 223
   varying sentence length, 221–22
   word placement, 218–19
Endnotes, 300–304
Ensure, assure, insure, 313
Enthused, 316
Equally as, 316
Especially, specially, 316
Euphony, 212–15
Exact same, 316
Example
   development by, 36–37, 40
   organization by, 20
Except, accept, 310
Exclamation point, 147
Expository essay, 11–12

Fact that, 316
Farther, further, 316–17
Faulty parallelism, 226–27
Fewer, less, 317
First person, 68
Flaunt, flout, 317
Footnotes, 300–304
Formal prose, 266–70
Former, latter, 317
Fragment, 88–92
Fused sentence, 94–95
Future perfect tense, 70
Future tense, 69

Gerund, 67
Good, well, 317

Had better, 317
Hanged, hung, 317
Helping verb, 70–71
Hyphen, 161–62

I.e., 315–16
Illusion, allusion, delusion, 318
Immanent, immiment, eminent, 316
Imperative mood, 68, 70
Imply, infer, 318
Indentation of quotations, 136–38
Independent clause, 77
Indicative mood, 68
Indirect questions, 145
Infinitive, 67
Informal prose, 266–68
Insure, assure, ensure, 313
Introductions, 275–83
   anecdote, 278
   contrast, 279–80
   example, 279

funnel method, 277–78
question, 282–83
quotation, 281–82
thesis statement, 283
Italics, 165–70
emphasis, 167
foreign words, 166
titles, 168–69
words referred to as words, 166–67
It's, its, 318

Jargon, 266

Latter, former, 317
Lay, lie, 318
Lead, led, 318
Lend, loan, 318–19
Less, fewer, 317
Like, as, 319
Linking verb, 103–104
Literally, 319
Loose, lose, 319

Mad, 319
Main clause, 77–78
May be, maybe, 319
May, can, 314
Media, 320
Misplaced modifier, 81
Modifiers, 80–84
dangling, 83
misplaced, 81
squinting, 82
Mood, 68

Moral, morale, 320
Must of, 320

Narration
development by, 36, 41
organization by, 21
Narrative essay, 12
Narrowing a topic, 5–10
Neither/nor, 228
No one, 320
Nonrestrictive phrase or clause, 116–17
Nor, 320
Not only/but also, 228
Notes, 300–304
Noun, defined, 65–67
collective noun, 102
Number, amount, 312
Numbers, 179–81

Organization, 19–24
cause and effect, 21
classification, 20
comparison and contrast, 21–24
example, 20
definition, 21
description, 21
narration, 21
process analysis, 21–22
Outline, 26–29

Parallelism, 225–33
faulty, 226–27

Parentheses, 153–57
　for less emphasis, 155
　to enclose entire sentence, 156–57
　to enclose numbers or letters in a list, 157
Parts of speech, 65–73
Passive verbs, 85–87
Past participle, 69
Past perfect tense, 69
Past subjunctive, 70
Past tense, 69
Period, 144–45
　after abbreviations, 145
　at end of sentence, 144–45
　to repair comma splice, 94
　to repair fused sentence, 94–95
Periodic sentence
　for emphasis, 219–20
Person, 67–68
Persuade, convince, 314
Possessives, 129–31
Possessive pronouns, 131–32
Precede, proceed, 320
Preposition, 71–72
Prepositional phrase, 76
Present perfect tense, 69
Present subjunctive, 70
Present tense, 69
Principal, principle, 320
Process analysis
　development by, 36
　organization by, 21–22
Progressive tenses, 70
Pronoun, defined, 71
　use for coherence, 50–51
Proper manuscript form, 297–308
Provided, provided that, providing, 321

Question
　direct, 145–46
　indirect, 145
Question mark
　in parentheses, 147
　in series, 146–47
　indentation, 137–38
　within quotation, 137
Quotation marks, 135–43
　direct quotation, 135–36
　jargon, etc., 141–42
　titles, 141
　words referred to as words, 141
　misuse, 142
　single, 137

Raise, rise, 321
Real, really, 321
Reason is because, 321
Refer to, allude to, 312
Repetition, 49–50, 234–43
　intentional, 234–37
　unnecessary, 237–38
Restrictive phrase or clause, 117
Revision, 59–62

Rhymes, unintentional, 214–15

Second person, 68
Semicolon, 124–28
  errors, 127–28
  in place of period, 125–27
  in series, 127
Sensor, censor, censer, censure, 314
Sentence, 74–79
  complex, 77
  compound, 76–77
  compound-complex, 79
  fragment, 88–92
  fused, 94–96
  periodic, 219–20
  simple, 74–76
"Sexist" writing, 293–96
Simple sentence, 74–76
Simplicity, 206–11
Slang, 265
Slash, 159–60
So . . . as, as . . . as, 342
Sometime, sometimes, some time, 321
Speaker tags, 120
Specially, especially, 316
Specificity, 255–62
Squinting modifier, 82
Stationary, stationery, 321
Style, 185–94
Subjunctive mood, 68
Subordinating conjunction, 77

Supposed to, 321
Synonyms
  for coherence, 51–53
  to avoid repetition, 239–43

Take, bring, 313
Tense, 69
Than, then, 321
That, which, 321
There, their, they're, 322
Thesis, 11–18
Third person, 68
Till, until, 'til, 322
Title
  ending in question mark, 146
  manuscript form, 299–300
To, too, two, 322
Tone, 200–205
Topic choice, 3–10
Topic sentence, 45–48
Toward, towards, 322
Transitional expression
  used for coherence, 53–58

Uninterested, disinterested, 315
Unity, 44
Unique, 322–23
until, 'til, till, 322
Usage, 309–24
Use, usage, utilize, 323
Used to, 323

Index

Variety, 244–54
  in sentence length and type, 244–54
  in subject, 252–53
Verb, defined, 67–71
  auxiliary, 70
  gerund, 67
  infinitive, 67
  mood, 68
  tense, 69
Virgule, 159–60
Voice, 85–87
  active, 85–87
  passive, 85–87

Well, good, 317
Were, where, 323
Which, that, 321
Who, whom, 323
Whose, who's, 324
Wordiness, 209–10
Would of, 324

Your, you're, 324

1
Realize that college paper topics are all around you.

2
Know your thesis from the start.

3
Whether or not you use a formal outline, always know where you're going.

4
Don't let the difficulties and frustrations of writing defeat you.

5
Develop every major point adequately.

6
Focus every paragraph on a single subtopic.

7
Make certain every sentence flows smoothly and logically from its predecessor.

8
Keep revising your paper till it is as good as you can make it.

9
Know the parts of speech and their relationships to one another.

10
Recognize simple, compound, and complex sentences, and be able to change sentences of one type to sentences of another type.

11
Place modifiers correctly.

12
Except in special instances, use the active voice.

13
Don't use sentence fragments unless you have good reason to do so.

14
Use appropriate punctuation to separate sentences.

15
Make certain that every verb agrees in number with its subject.

16
Make certain that every pronoun agrees in number with its antecedent.

17
Use commas thoughtfully.

18
Use the semicolon to separate two independent clauses that enjoy a close logical relationship.

19
Use the apostrophe to indicate possessives and (in informal prose) contractions.

20
Mark quotations carefully.

21
Use end punctuation precisely, making certain not to use periods and question marks together or to overuse exclamation points.

22
Use a colon to separate an independent clause from the set of words that it introduces.